CITYSPOTS
ATHENS

Mike Gerrard

Written by Mike Gerrard
Original photography by Tony Gervis
Front cover photography courtesy of Alamy Images

Produced by 183 Books
Design/layout/maps: Chris Lane and Lee Biggadike
Editorial/project management: Stephen York

Published by Thomas Cook Publishing
A division of Thomas Cook Tour Operations Limited
PO Box 227, Units 15/16, Coningsby Road
Peterborough PE3 8SB, United Kingdom
email: books@thomascook.com
www.thomascookpublishing.com
+44 (0)1733 416477

First edition © 2006 Thomas Cook Publishing
Text © 2006 Thomas Cook Publishing
Maps © 2006 Thomas Cook Publishing

ISBN-13: 978-1-84157-589-6
ISBN-10: 1-84157-589-5
Project Editor: Kelly Anne Pipes
Production/DTP: Steven Collins

Printed and bound in Spain by GraphyCems

CONTENTS

SYMBOLS & ABBREVIATIONS

The following symbols are used throughout this book:

☎ telephone	🖷 fax	✉ email	🌐 website address
✉ address	⏱ opening times	🚉 public transport connections	

The following symbols are used on the maps:
- 🅸 Tourist Information Office
- ✈ Airport

Hotels and restaurants are graded by approximate price as follows:
€ budget price **€€** mid-range price **€€€** expensive

24-HOUR CLOCK

All times in this book are given in the 24-hour clock system used widely in Europe and in most international transport timetables.

 Military symmetry at the Changing of the Guard

Introduction

There has never been a better time to visit Athens. Even before the advent of the 2004 Olympics, there was a new buzz about the city – new bars, Michelin stars, boutique hotels, run-down areas regenerated and the city centre getting more and more traffic-free zones. As the Olympics approached, the frenzy increased, and now they are over the feel-good factor remains.

Athens was always a good place to be, but its fans and friends had to warn first-time visitors that it did have its drawbacks. There was too much traffic. Expect good food but not great food. The basically one-line subway system was … well, functional. Getting from the airport could be a hassle and a chance to find out the truth in what someone once said – that 90 per cent of Greeks are friendly and honest, and the rest went to Athens and became taxi drivers.

OK, so it's still impossible to get a taxi, the buses are as crowded as ever and it takes a brave soul to drive a car in Athens. But the new metro system is sleek and still spreading, traffic is banned from an increasing number of areas, the quality of Greek food and wine has soared hugely in the last ten years and the city is now one of Europe's most vibrant capitals.

Despite all these changes, it has lost none of its soul or its sense of history. The magnificent Parthenon still dominates the city centre skyline, reminding every new arrival that Greece was having a Golden Age while Parisians were still living in mud huts. It's the birthplace of democracy, of philosophy and drama, and this link with the past is still there and visible, every time you turn a street corner.

Athens is very much a city for people. People still live in the city centre, and it shows. Where other cities have been taken over by office blocks and international chain stores, Athens still has corner shops and neighbourhood cafés. It's a city with a human face, and the face usually has a smile on it.

○ *Restaurants and cafés are the centre of neighbourhood social life*

When to go

CLIMATE

It's surprising to discover that it rains in Athens on roughly 100 days each year. But sun-lovers shouldn't let that put them off, as on many of those days it's no more than an occasional light shower, and most of the rainfall is in the winter. Hardly a drop falls from July to September.

The worst times to visit are probably from late July through to early September. The *average* temperature in midsummer is 32° C (90° F), which means on many days it exceeds that. Summer heatwaves are a common phenomenon and although the city has done an enormous amount in the past few years to reduce the problem of traffic congestion, which adds to the unpleasantness by helping create a summer smog, it hasn't got rid of it completely. The middle of summer is best avoided if at all possible.

Spring and autumn, on the other hand, are perfect times to see Athens. You might be unlucky and get some rain, but chances are the skies will be blue and the temperature pleasant. The average in May and October is 20° C (68° F). Even in winter, don't rule Athens out. Skies can still be bright blue and the weather mild. January is the coldest month, when the average drops to 9° C (48° F).

ANNUAL EVENTS

February/March

Carnival Carnival is not as big in Greece as it is in, say, Venice or the Caribbean, but they do still celebrate it. You'll find music in the streets of Athens, especially around the Plaka district, with children in costume and people hitting each other on the head with plastic hammers. The big day is the Sunday immediately before the start of

Lent, and this falls seven weeks before Easter Sunday (see page 12 for dates).

Independence Day 25 March sees the first really big event of the year, celebrating the start of the revolt against the years of Turkish rule in Greece. There are parades and festivities, especially outside the Greek Parliament building on Syntagma Square.

April
Easter This is the biggest religious celebration in Greece and a time when it's a joy to be there, whether you're religious or not. There are religious processions through the streets, shown live on TV, and Athens has one of the biggest Easter celebrations in the country. Greek Easter usually falls in April, though not always, and it doesn't usually coincide with the dates of the western European Easter (see page 12).

May/June
Labour Day 1 May is a public holiday and there are workers' parades through the streets.

Whit Monday Fifty days after Easter Sunday, the Greeks are at it again with a national holiday and more street parades and parties, both public and private.

The Athens Festival Beginning in late May and running through till early October (though dates vary slightly: check website for up-to-date information) is this big annual arts festival – bigger than ever in 2006, as it celebrates its 50th anniversary. As well as the best in Greek classical arts, recent visitors have included the Bolshoi Ballet,

● *Rockwave has become a fixture in the Athenian festival calendar*

the English National Ballet and the Berlin Symphony Orchestra.
Many events take place in the ancient Odeon (Theatre) of Herodes
Atticus (see page 64). A special box office is usually opened for the
duration of the festival. ● Stadiou 4. ● 210 928 2900.
Ⓦ www.greekfestival.gr

The Lycabettus Festival This comes under the Athens Festival
umbrella, but events in the outdoor theatre on Lykavittos Hill are
more modern. In 2005 Franz Ferdinand was one of the many bands
that played, and there are contemporary theatre and dance
performances too, but also a few traditional Greek musical and
performance offerings. Ⓦ www.greekfestival.gr

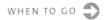

Music Day 21–23 June is when Athens joins in a European celebration of music with hundreds of groups and solo artists playing at venues throughout the city. Jazz, rock, traditional music: everything from children's choirs to the Scissor Sisters.
Ⓦ www.musicday.gr

Rockwave Moby, Twisted Sister and Black Sabbath were among the 2005 headliners at this now annual rock music festival that takes place at the Terra Vibe centre, out of the city centre on the Lamia road. Expect acrobats, bungee jumping and other fun stuff too.
Ⓣ 210 882 0426. Ⓦ www.didimusic.gr/rockwave

PUBLIC HOLIDAYS

Shops and some public services might close down for public holidays, but restaurants, museums and public transport generally keep operating. There are no hard and fast rules in Athens, though. People do what they feel like doing on the day.

New Year's Day 1 Jan

Epiphany 6 Jan

Independence Day 25 Mar

First Monday in Lent (Shrove Monday) Feb

Good Friday & Easter Monday Mar/Apr (see page 12 for 2006 and 2007 Easter dates)

Labour Day 1 May

Whit Monday 5 June 1006, 28 May 2007

Feast of the Assumption 15 Aug

Ochi Day (see page 15) 28 Oct

Christmas 25–26 Dec

Greek Easter

Easter in Athens is one of the best times to visit the city. Not only is the weather usually starting to warm up but for the Greeks Easter is the big feast day of the year, much more so than Christmas, New Year or any other event. It is celebrated everywhere, from the tiniest village through to here, in the nation's capital of 4 million people. The Orthodox Church's Easter only coincides with the Western Church's Easter every few years, so it is important to check the dates before arranging to travel: in 2006 Easter Sunday in Greece is on 23 April and in 2007 it's on 8 April.

The build-up begins on the Wednesday before Easter, when churches are cleaned and the flower decoration of the biers that will carry a statue of Christ through the streets begins. Pop into any open church door and see what preparations are being made. Everyone is welcome.

The parishioners from each church come together to prepare for the big weekend, and there will be many small processions throughout the city, as well as larger ones from the major churches. The first procession is on Friday evening. As it starts to get dark the funeral bier is carried from the church and paraded through the nearby streets. Parishioners follow on, and others watch from windows and doorways, sprinkling holy water liberally around.

Saturday evening sees the main service of the week, building up to midnight when lights in the church are put out. The priest then lights a candle, from which the worshippers in turn light their own candles, then leave the church producing an effect like a river of light, flowing from the church doors. People then try to get home without the candle blowing out, which brings good luck for the coming year.

Once home they eat the traditional *magaritsa* soup, made from lamb offal, rice and lemon.

Easter Sunday is a day of joy, and a day for families to get together. Lambs are roasted, and you may be able to find some on the restaurant menus that day. Christ is Risen, and the year can begin. You don't have to be religious or Christian to be moved by the Greek Easter experience.

● *Easter processions take place all over Athens*

History

If there's one thing Athens has in abundance, it's history. There were people living here, on and around the Acropolis, some 5000 years ago. By the 6th century BC it was a flourishing and forward-thinking city, and had introduced a revolutionary form of governing system with decisions made by citizens – they called it *democratia*, 'rule by the people'. As yet no women or slaves could vote, but nevertheless the system was as enlightened as any in the world.

Democracy worked. Little over a hundred years later an era known as the Golden Age of Pericles began. Pericles was probably the greatest statesman that Athens has ever seen, and it's thanks to his vision that the Parthenon on top of the Acropolis, and many other fine buildings, were built. He encouraged the arts and philosophy too, and this was the time when Sophocles, Aeschylus and Euripides were all working. European drama was not just being born but developing, its boundaries already being pushed by experimentation.

After the death of Pericles and a period of unrest for Athens following defeat in the Peloponnesian war against Sparta, Alexander the Great was born and Greece had the most powerful and extensive empire it has ever known. But all empires eventually wane, and by 200 BC the Romans has arrived and were to rule for 500 years. Their legacy is everywhere, including the Roman Agora, or marketplace, and Hadrian's Arch, still standing almost 1900 years later.

After the Romans Athens saw the Franks and the Venetians taking control, and then the most significant of all – the Turks. This detested period lasted from 1453 until the start of the War of Independence in 1821. Relations between the two Balkan neighbours haven't improved much since, though recently the antipathy has mellowed slightly.

In 1832 Otto of Bavaria became the first king of the modern Greek state. Why Bavaria? Because the new country was still considered unstable, especially when its first Prime Minister Ioannis Kapodistrias was assassinated in Nafplion. Russia, Britain and France had all been involved in the birth of modern Greece, and it was through them that a suitable monarch was found.

In 1940 Italy demanded access to Greek ports, to which the Greek leader Metaxas famously replied 'Ochi' (No) – commemorated on 28 October each year. Despite a heroic defence, Greece was occupied by the Axis powers; at the end of World War II there was a short but vicious Civil War between monarchists and communists. However, the monarchy survived until 1967, when a military junta seized power and King Constantine fled into exile. The Colonels ruled with military ruthlessness until 1974, when the people of Athens, particularly its young students, overthrew the dictatorship. There was no triumphant return for the exiled king, however, as a referendum saw a majority vote for a return to a Greek republic.

In 1981 Greece joined the then European Community, now the European Union, and changes started to happen. The city of Athens became much more European in outlook. Its young people travelled more, and brought back with them a desire for some of the style, the fashions, the food and the wine that they had experienced elsewhere. In 1985 Athens was Europe's first ever Cultural Capital – fittingly, as the idea of Cultural Capitals had been hatched by the Greek actress-turned-politician, Melina Mercouri.

In 2004 the Olympics came to Athens and found a city that had been regenerated and was self-confident, with perhaps just a feeling that another Golden Age might be beginning.

Lifestyle

Like all Greeks, Athenians love life. They are typical Mediterraneans, with an outgoing nature, a love of conversation and company and a complete disregard for both authority and time. If you're in Athens for business meetings then there's a better chance that people will be punctual, but for social encounters, 20.00 can mean 20.30 or even later. But why worry? It's the meeting that matters, not the timing of it.

There's an agreeable chaos about Athens, a little drama on every street corner, but everything works out ... eventually, more or less. The Olympics was the perfect example of that. There were scandals and strikes and delays and much shouting and arm-waving amid concerns that things would never be ready on time, but the Athenians got there in the end.

● *Athenian lifestyle is outdoor and gregarious*

Athens is also one of the safest cities in the world. The vast majority of Greeks are honest and trustworthy, and crime rates are very low. Overcharging a tourist does not count as dishonesty, that's a way of life, but if you ever leave a bag behind in a shop or restaurant, it will be looked after for you till you return. Obviously if you walk down dark alleys late at night you're asking for trouble, but apart from the obvious precautions you're as safe in Athens as anywhere in the world.

There is one regular nuisance, but it's easily avoided. If you hear someone call out to you in the street and say, 'Do you have the time?' it's better to feign deafness and walk on. They may seem perfectly polite and friendly, but if you stop they will then ask where you're from and hold you in conversation. This then leads on to an invitation to stay at their cousin's hotel, an attempt to sell you something, or pick your pocket, or a scam of some kind. It is best to ignore them from the start. Such people are a tiny minority in Athens, but they are there and they are con-men. Apart from little irritations like this, relax and enjoy that Greek hospitality in a land where the word for 'stranger' and 'guest' are one and the same.

NAME THAT PLACE
Greek place names can be confusing till you're used to them. There is the original name, obviously in the Greek alphabet, and there will be several versions in the Roman alphabet, depending on how the Greek has been transliterated. Several Greek letters have no direct equivalent, so the town of Delphi can also be written as Delfi. The island of Halki might be Chalki or Khalki. Athens is pretty safe: in the Greek language it is Athinai.

Culture

You cannot escape Athens' great history, and nor should you want to. Even the second- and third-time visitor will find themselves drawn back to the Acropolis (see page 60) and the National Archaeological Museum (see page 79), and you don't need to be especially interested in the past to appreciate both of them.

There are many other ancient treasures waiting to be discovered too, and if you are on a short weekend visit you will have to be selective. The Goulandris Museum of Cycladic Art (see page 92) should be near the top of most lists, showing how some of the ancient art forms are as modern as tomorrow. The nearby Benaki Museum (see page 91) has several floors of ancient and more recent artefacts, and within two minutes of here are also the National Gallery (see page 94), the Byzantine Museum (see page 92) and the War Museum (see page 94) too.

A whole day could be spent just visiting the museums in the Plaka district alone – the Museum of Greek Folk Art (see page 71), the Kanellopoulos Museum (see page 68), the wonderful Museum of Greek Musical Instruments (see page 70) and the small but delightful Museum of Greek Children's Art (see page 146).

If you ignore the museums and focus on the archaeological sites, that could be another day that's both full and fascinating. Most of these are in and around the Plaka district too, including the Agora (see page 66) and, a short walk away, the ancient Keramikos cemetery, with its small museum (see page 67).

It's hard for today's artists and artisans to escape the past that's

● *The National Archaeological Museum is a must for anyone with an interest in Classical Greece*

OPENING HOURS

Opening hours at museums and sites can never be totally relied on. A lot of them change from year to year, and even within a year after the official hours have been announced. They may be unexpectedly closed. It's best to check with a current local source like a newspaper or magazine, if possible.

all around them, and many incorporate aspects of the city's history and myths into their work. There's a flourishing literary scene, with the work of Athenian-based Greek writers being increasingly translated into other languages. Athenian ceramic artists and photographers are also highly skilled, and there are plenty of galleries exhibiting their work, and of talented modern painters, sculptors and mixed-media artists too.

Athens can't hope to rival cities like Paris or Milan when it comes to high culture, though its summer festival (see page 9) is as good as any and allows the city to showcase its own dance, music and theatre companies.

It's for more popular culture that most people enjoy Athens, though, and here it really comes into its own. Traditional Greek music is alive and well in the hands of contemporary musicians, and these and some old hands play in the city's many bars and clubs. You can also find numerous rock, blues and jazz venues which feature local as well as visiting musicians. Arm yourself with one of the several local listings magazines and be prepared to go anywhere but the tourist haunts of the Plaka.

◐ *Athens' most charming church – the Little Mitropolis*

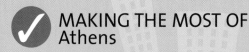

Shopping

WHERE TO GO

It's with down-to-earth shopping rather than department stores that Athens really scores. Its street markets and food stores, where the locals shop, are where you really find good value and genuine local items. There are many of the familiar international names such as Lacoste, Next and Benetton, most of which can be found on the pedestrianised Ermou, the main street that runs west from Syntagma Square. Panepestimiou is another main shopping street. Here, and in some of the arcades and streets running off it, you'll find many of the upmarket jewellers. Kolonaki is the district to head

for if you're interested in antiques and art galleries, while the Plaka is where the souvenir shops congregate. The flea market around Monastiraki Square is unmissable, especially on Sunday morning. Then it can get so packed that it can be hard to move, but the stalls have an amazing mix of bric-a-brac, antiques, clothes, old books ... everything under the sun.

WHAT TO BUY

Leather is always a good buy in Athens, while gold and silver are usually more affordable here than elsewhere. These range from big

International names abound around Ermou

USEFUL SHOPPING PHRASES

What time do the shops open/close?
Τι ώρα ανοίγουν/κλείνουν τα καταστήματα;
Ti ora anigun/klinun ta katastimata?

How much is this?
Πόσο κάνει αυτό;
Poso kani afto?

Can I try this on?
Μπορώ να το δοκιμάσω;
Boro na to dokimaso?

My size is ...
Το νούμερό μου είναι ...
To numero mu ine ...

I'll take this one, thank you
Θα πάρω αυτό εδώ, ευχαριστώ
Tha paro afto edo, efharisto

designer names like Ilias Lalaounis to small one-man stores found in the back streets north of Ermou near the Syntagma end. Greek food and drink is also an enjoyable buy, especially local olive oil, Greek wines, cheap spirits and mountain honey. To find the best choices, head for the streets south of Omonia Square, in and around the fascinating Central Market with its meat, fish and food stalls.

Take a look in the museum shops too. Some of the reproductions of museum items are beautifully done, and there are often contemporary art and craft items on sale too. Icon paintings are uniquely Greek objects. You can find mass reproductions in some of the souvenir shops, but hand-painted icons are still made using traditional techniques and materials. Look in the streets around the Cathedral to find these. In most shops the prices are fixed, but elsewhere, especially in the markets, don't be afraid to do a bit of haggling.

● *Icons make perfect souvenirs*

Eating & drinking

It wasn't very long ago that Athens only had a handful of really exceptional restaurants, the vast majority being good-value places with similar menus, and some rather over-priced options trying to lure the tourists in the Plaka. That's no longer the case. Standards have risen, Michelin stars have arrived and it is as easy and as expensive to have a gourmet meal in Athens as in any other European capital. However, it is still possible to find those good-value meals, and if you are in Athens and sticking to a budget your money will stretch much further here than almost anywhere else.

The only thing that hasn't changed is that the Plaka still has a number of places where the food is mediocre. There's a simple rule for dealing with this: never eat anywhere which pays someone to stand outside trying to persuade you to come inside. It isn't an infallible rule, but it's right more often than it's wrong. The best places in the Plaka are a handful of simple basement *tavérnes*. If you have to go down steps to get in, the place will probably be good.

If you haven't set out to eat anywhere in particular but enjoy walking around trying to decide where to eat, head not for the Plaka but for the neighbouring Psyrri district to the north-west. This buzzes with ouzeries, bars and restaurants and is where the Athenians go to eat. Many places only have Greek menus but don't let that put you off. Most staff speak English and can tell you what they've got.

LOCAL SPECIALITIES

Some of the best Greek food is the *meze*, the Greek version of Spanish tapas. They include typical starter dishes such as *taramasalata*, *tzatziki* (a yoghurt/cucumber/garlic dip) and aubergine salad, but many more unusual dishes are also often

RESTAURANT CATEGORIES
In this book the approximate price bands into which restaurants fall are based on the average cost of a three-course evening meal for one person, excluding drinks, indicated by these symbols:
€ under €20 €€ €20–40 €€€ Over €40

available. They come on small plates and you can make an entire meal from them, if you order several. You can ask the waiter for a selection of *meze* for one or two people, or more, but make sure you're hungry, as the Greeks have big appetites!

There are countless inexpensive tavernas in Athens where you can get good Greek staples such as moussaka, stuffed peppers, stuffed aubergines, lamb and beef stews, grilled chicken and pork. They're often very good, if a little unexciting. Greek food is much more varied than that, these days, and more sophisticated. Be adventurous. Head for the Psyri and Gaza districts. Ask at your hotel for recommendations. Check our recommendations. But don't simply walk into the first place where a waiter standing outside beckons you in. They never approach Athenians in that way, so be wary.

⬤ *Outdoor eating is one of the great pleasures of a stay in Athens*

TYPES OF RESTAURANT

The word restaurant (*estiatório* in Greek) is in common use in
Athens and mostly refers to a slightly more upmarket eating place
than a *tavérna*. The taverna is usually less formal, the kind of place
where you might be invited into the kitchen to see the day's dishes
rather than choose from a menu. Tavernas are generally cheaper,
too. Then there are ouzeries, which serve the local aniseed-flavoured
drink, ouzo, with snacks and sometimes full meals – more akin to a
Spanish tapas bar. *Psistariés* are places that specialise in grilled food,
and *psarotavérnes* focus on fish and seafood.

BREAKFAST

Hotel room rates sometimes include breakfast and sometimes
don't. Some hotels serve excellent breakfasts in continental fashion,
with coffee, fresh juice, fresh breads and croissants, cold meats,
cheeses, fruit and yoghurt with honey. Others serve a perfunctory
meal of dried toast, watery orange juice and cereal. If that's the case
then you should head straight out to a neighbourhood café and
have something there instead.

PICNICS

Athens is not a great city for picnics. The National Garden (see page 88)
is the best spot, away from the traffic and with lots of benches and
greenery around. If you want a snack for there, or to take on a day trip,
then go shopping near the Central Market, south of Omonia Square.
Here you'll find olives, bread, cheeses, dips and fruit, to put together a
tasty meal. Pies are popular with locals, and you can buy these at shops
on almost every street. Like fast food anywhere, they range from the
delicious to the dismal, but a good hot and fresh spinach or cheese pie
is a cheap and filling treat.

EATING TIMES

Athenians eat late. Starting lunch at 14.00–15.00 is normal, and dinner before 21.00 is something only visitors do. Places are open much earlier than this, to cater to the needs of visitors, but if you want the real Athenian experience you'll adjust to their eating times.

TIPPING

Your bill in a restaurant will usually include a service charge, so there is no need to add on a tip. If no service charge has been added, then leaving 10–15 per cent or making up the bill to the nearest round amount is normal. It's also customary to leave any loose change or small notes on the table for whoever does the clearing away.

USEFUL DINING PHRASES

I would like a table for ... people
Θα ήθελα ένα τραπέζι για ... άτομα
Tha ithela ena trapezi gia ... atoma

Waiter/waitress!
Γκαρσόν/Σερβιτόρα!
Garson/Servitora!

May I have the bill, please?
Μπορώ να έχω το λογαριασμό, παρακαλώ;
Boro na eho to logariasmo, parakalo?

I am a vegetarian.
Does this contain meat?
Είμαι χορτοφάγος.
Περιέχει κρέας αυτό;
Ime hortofawos. Periehi kreas afto?

Where is the toilet (restroom) please?
Πού είναι η τουαλέτα, παρακαλώ;
Pu ine i tualeta, parakalo?

Entertainment & nightlife

THEATRE, DANCE & CLASSICAL

While Athens has a lively theatre scene and a National Theatre company, most performances are in Greek. You might get to see a visiting theatre group, if you check the listings while you're there. There is also a Greek National Opera company, and several halls putting on classical concerts. Dance is popular too, from contemporary work to classical ballet to Greek traditional dance, notably at the Dora Stratou Theatre at the foot of Filopappou Hill.

SOUND & LIGHT

One of the most popular night-time entertainments for visitors to Athens is the Sound & Light Show, which tells the history of the Acropolis and of the city. It's a very impressive and dramatic production and takes place in different languages on different evenings. The seating is at the foot of the Pnyx Hill, naturally on the Acropolis side. This is also where you can buy tickets and check programme times.

BARS, DISCOS & CLUBS

Athenians like to have a good time and the city has as many bars, clubs and discos as anywhere else. These range from intimate venues which might play a little soft jazz to huge barns of discos pumping out hip-hop at shattering levels. Because of the noise factor, and the summer heat, during the hot months some clubs close down because the customers prefer to head out to the open-air venues in the city's beach-resort suburbs.

In the bars and clubs every kind of music is catered for (jazz, blues, rock, reggae, '6os, world music) but it's advisable to check the local listings magazines, because while some clubs are devoted to one kind of music, other have different styles on different nights. There are fewer choices available in the summer, partly due to the air-conditioning question and partly due to musicians going out to the Greek islands to work the much busier tourist resorts there.

CINEMAS

There are plenty of cinemas all over Athens, showing international releases in the original language, with Greek sub-titles. They are fairly inexpensive, and programmes can be found in listings magazines (see below). In summer many close down, unless they have good air-conditioning, and open-air cinemas spring up to take their place. These tend to show second-run movies and old black-and-white films, and are very much social occasions. People talk a lot, as they are not listening to the foreign soundtrack, which can make it hard for foreign visitors who are desperately trying to hear what's going on! Late-night showings usually have the sound turned down anyway, to avoid disturbing the neighbourhood.

TICKETS & INFORMATION

The easiest way to get concert tickets is to go into almost any of the big central record shops and buy them there. They are also a good source of information, with adverts and flyers for concerts and clubs. The best source of entertainment information is *Athinorama* magazine, published every Friday. This is in Greek but is still useful, as names of films, bands, programme times etc. are all in English. It helps to know the days of the week in Greek – see page 152. Otherwise the English-language *Athens Daily News* can also be checked, although it is less comprehensive. The Friday edition does carry more detailed listings for the weekend.

Sport & relaxation

SPECTATOR SPORTS

Visitors don't usually go to Athens for the sports, but there are as many opportunities here as in any other city. The two biggest sports in Greece are basketball and football, and it can be great fun to try and take in a match if you're there during the season. You should be able to get tickets unless it's a big derby game or important league clash. The biggest basketball team is Panathinaikos, who play in the Maroussi suburb, easily reachable on metro line 1. The two top soccer teams are AEK Athens and Panathinaikos, both playing at the new **Olympic Stadium** (🚇 Metro: Irini) while awaiting new grounds.

AEK Athens 🛈 210 612 1371. 🌐 www.aekfc.gr

Panathinaikos (football) 🛈 210 809 3630. 🌐 www.pao.gr

Panathinaikos (basketball) 🛈 210 610 7160. 🌐 www.paobc.gr

BEACHES & WATERSPORTS

Most people think of Athens for its archaeological sites and all the typical attractions of a city, but few people realise that within half an hour of the Acropolis you could be lying on the beach. The coast east of Athens has a string of resorts, which merge into each other and feel more like city suburbs. Several of the beaches have won EU Blue Flag awards for cleanliness and offer lots of facilities. Naturally they get busy, so try to avoid weekends if you prefer peaceful sunbathing. Access is easy and cheap if you can master the public transport system, as the beaches are all served by buses or trams. You could also take a taxi to and from the closer beaches. The closest is at Edem, which is sandy, free and has a few eating places, but if you want watersports and beach sports facilities then take a bus to the suburbs of Voula and Vouliagmeni. There is a mix of public and private beaches here so you may have to pay, and some can be quite pricey, so you might want to shop around.

OTHER ACTIVITIES

There are plenty of gyms, tennis pitches and swimming pools in the city. For further information ask at the tourist office (see page 151). If you like hiking and want to enjoy the countryside around Athens, the easiest way is to call in at Trekking Hellas in the Plaka and see what tours they have on offer.

Trekking Hellas ⓐ Filellinon 7. ⓣ 210 331 0323. ⓦ www.trekking.gr

◗ Athens' two football teams share the Olympic Stadium pitch

Accommodation

Travellers to Athens can be grateful to the Olympics. The city has always had a good range of places to stay, especially in the low/medium price brackets, but before the 2004 Olympics many new hotels opened while others, aided by government grants, were encouraged to upgrade their facilities. The result is an even better choice of accommodation, from cheap hostels, through amazingly inexpensive mid-price hotels to the kind of five-star chains and modern chic boutique hotels that were previously lacking.

The wide range of choice means that you should really aim to be right in the city centre, unless you have a specific reason for basing yourself further out. Athens is easy to get around on foot, so look for somewhere close to Syntagma or Omonia Squares, or to the Plaka. You can be right in the heart of the Plaka and still have a good choice of places at different prices. For reasons of space and history, hotels right in the centre tend to be smaller and cheaper than more modern and more luxurious hotels, which had to be built slightly further out.

There are usually plenty of hotel rooms to go round, except in midsummer when, despite the prospect of intense heat, hotels can be full. At other times you needn't worry too much if you arrive in Athens without a booking. Head for the Plaka and walk around. Travel agents can also help, and are a much better bet than the

PRICE RATINGS

The hotel price ratings used in this book are based on the cost of a double room per night.

€ Under €100 €€ €100–200 €€€ Over€200.

tourist information offices. You may not get the best price doing it this way, however, so if time allows, search on the internet, check out hotels' official websites, and look for bargain offers.

HOTEL CATEGORIES

Greek hotels are officially graded and put into one of six categories, from Luxury and then down from A to E. The tourist police check prices each year, and these must be displayed in each room. That's when you'll find out how much of a discount you managed to get! If cost is a factor, bear in mind that Athens is still quite cheap, and that no rating system is infallible. There are some very comfortable and inexpensive hotels that are in the C category simply because you may not have a telephone in your room, or there may not be a balcony.

HOTELS

Acropolis House € Converted 19th-century mansion much liked by budget travellers, in a quiet Plaka street where there are other options if this hotel is full. Not all rooms are en suite in this simple hotel. ⓐ Kodrou 6. ⓣ 210 322 2344. ⓕ 210 324 4143.

Adonis € Modern, small and friendly, this clean and well run hotel is on the edge of the Plaka and breakfast on the rooftop terrace with its Acropolis views is not a bad way to start each day. ⓐ Kodrou 3. ⓣ 210 324 9737. ⓕ 210 323 1602.

Attalos € Recently refurbished, and with exceptionally friendly staff, this is one of the best bargains in town, halfway between Omonia Square and the Plaka. Rooftop bar has Acropolis views. ⓐ Athinas 29. ⓣ 210 321 2801. ⓦ www.attalos.gr

Pella Inn € In the bustling Monastiraki bazaar area, this family hotel is very simple but clean and a friendly place to stay, with easy access to all the best parts of central Athens. Some of the rooms on upper floors have Acropolis views to rival any five-star hotel's. ❷ Ermou 104. ❶ 210 325 0598. Ⓦ www.pella-inn.gr

Hotel Plaka €€ Extremely comfortable and stylish hotel which would be twice the price in London or Paris. Some rooms on upper floors have Acropolis views, if you can get one. ❷ Kapnikareas 7. ❶ 210 322 2096. ❶ 210 322 2412. Ⓦ www.plakahotel.gr

St George Lycabettus €€ Boutique-style five-star hotel with great location on the Lykavittos Hill in Kolonaki, with a rooftop pool and views towards the Acropolis. ❷ Kleomenous 2. ❶ 210 729 0711. Ⓦ www.sglycabettus.gr

Athens Acropol €€€ With its designer bars and modern artworks in public spaces, this chic hotel helped transform the previously dowdy area around Omonia Square. Popular with business travellers for its facilities, including fast internet access in all rooms. ❷ Pireas 1. ❶ 210 528 2100. Ⓦ www.grecotelcity.gr

Athens Hilton €€€ Unarguably one of the city's best modern hotels, the Hilton has recently been restored and redesigned to produce the ultimate in contemporary comfort. Its rooftop Galaxy Bar has become one of *the* places to have a drink. Well-placed near the National Gallery, a few minutes from Syntagma Square. ❷ Vasilissis Sofias 46. ❶ 210 728 1000. ❶ 210 728 1111. Ⓦ www.athens.hilton.com

---

● *There's a good choice of accommodation around Syntagma Square*

Grande Bretagne €€€ As much a historic site as a hotel, this *grande dame* of Athens hotels is right on Syntagma Square. Built in 1862 as an annexe to the royal family's summer palace, it has been recently refurbished. Even if you don't stay here, at least look inside.
🅰 Syntagma Square. 🕿 210 333 0000. 🆆 www.grandebretagne.gr

SELF-CATERING

This is not an easy option in Athens, where hotel prices have always been inexpensive, but apartments can be tracked down. The best bet is to ask in the travel agents around Syntagma Square and the Plaka.

YOUTH HOSTELS

YHA € There is only one official youth hostel in Athens, although several hotels advertise themselves as hostels and offer cheap dorm accommodation. The YHA is conveniently located between the city's two train stations and Omonia Square, an easy walk into the centre.
🅰 Victor Hugo 16. 🕿 210 523 4170. 🅵 210 523 4015.
🆆 www.interland.gr/athenshostel

CAMPING

Although there are three campsites within striking distance of the city centre, the best option is:
Camping Nea Kifissia In the pleasant northern suburb of Kifissia, where there is a metro connection to the city centre. 🕿 210 807 5579.

◗ *Luxury in a central location – the Hotel Grande Bretagne*

THE BEST OF ATHENS

The longer you can spend in Athens, the better. Those with only a few hours often have no time to do anything but wander the streets and see the noisy traffic, which is definitely not the best side of the city! If your time is limited, make a plan (see suggestions overleaf). Even in one day you won't do justice to the city's two main sights, the Acropolis and the National Archaeological Museum, and if this is all you have then maybe pick one or the other, depending on the weather. You can book coach tours of the city but given the traffic you are far better off exploring and discovering the city for yourself, unless you have mobility problems. For the best attractions for children, see pages 145–147.

TOP 10 ATTRACTIONS

- **The Acropolis** One of the world's greatest ancient sites (see page 60).

- **National Archaeological Museum** The greatest collection of Greek antiquities anywhere (see page 79).

- **The Plaka** This district below the Acropolis is unashamedly touristy, but still attractive and Athenian too (see page 64).

- **Psyrri** Visitors go to the Plaka, but Athenians flock to the Psyrri district, right next door, for an evening out (see page 72).

- **Goulandris Museum of Cycladic Art** A specialist collection of beautiful objects, beautifully displayed (see page 92).

- **Syntagma Square** The heart of Athens, in front of the Parliament buildings (see page 84).

- **The Changing of the Guard** This choreographed ritual is fascinating to watch (see page 44).

- **Monastiraki Flea Market** See it on Sunday morning if you can, though there's always something happening here (see page 23).

- **The Olympic Stadiums** The stadium for the 1896 Olympics is right in the city centre, and a visit to the 2004 stadium shows you how times have changed (see pages 32 and 89).

- **Museum of Greek Musical Instruments** A small but fun museum, with plenty to see ... and to listen to (see page 70).

🔽 *The Acropolis offers great panoramas of the city*

Your brief guide to seeing and experiencing the best of Athens, depending on the time you have available.

HALF-DAY: ATHENS IN A HURRY

You can't see it all so don't even try: focus on the Acropolis. Approach it from the south side, and go early if you can. The site and museum will take you at least an hour. Turn right when you exit, down into the Plaka district, where there are plenty of places to have a coffee or glass of wine and buy souvenirs. A little further on is Monastiraki Square, for a touch of authentic Athenian street life.

1 DAY: TIME TO SEE A LITTLE MORE

If you have a full day, consider your afternoon options after the half-day suggested above. In winter and on holidays the National Archaeological Museum closes at 15.00, not giving time to squeeze this in. In summer it stays open later, so head there. Most other museums and archaeological sites close at 15.00 all year round, so if there is one you want to see, go straight there after the Acropolis and save your strolling and shopping for the afternoon. With only time for one evening meal, head for Psyrri.

2–3 DAYS: SHORT CITY BREAK

If you have a few days, save the National Archaeological Museum for the second morning after trying out our one-day programme above. After a few hours here you may have museum fatigue, but outdoor sites such as the Roman Agora or Keramikos Cemetery can still be enjoyed. Visit Lykavittos hill, too, for good views over the Acropolis. You could also dine here in the evening, and enjoy the night-time city scene.

LONGER: ENJOYING ATHENS TO THE FULL

If you have more than three days, make use of the extra time by exploring further afield. Take the metro to the bustling port area at Pireas (see page 98) and have a seafood lunch, or catch a bus out to Cape Sounion (see page 105) for the sunset. A trip to Delphi (page 123) or Nafplion (page 129) will take a full day, as will a visit to the nearest Greek islands (page 110).

◯ *Seeing the Acropolis by night is an unforgettable experience*

Something for nothing

Athens is one of Europe's cheapest capital cities, and while you could spend a lot of money by booking the best accommodation and restaurants, most of the attractions and general prices are still inexpensive for visitors. And if you do want to see Athens on a budget, it's quite easy with a little thought and planning.

Syntagma Square is at the very centre of Athens, and here each day you can enjoy the almost hypnotic Changing of the Guard

⬇ *Views like this come free of charge*

ceremony in front of the Parliament building at the top of the square. The guards in their traditional costumes are very photogenic, and the ceremony takes place hourly at about 20 minutes before the hour. The Sunday morning changing is the main ceremonial one of the week, with full orchestral accompaniment, and though this is often said to be at 11.00, it usually begins at 10.40, like all the others, so don't be late.

From Syntagma it's a short walk through the Kolonaki district (expensive but window-shopping costs nothing!) to the foot of Lykavittos Hill. Walk to the top up the winding paths for the best free view in the city, of the Parthenon sitting on top of the Acropolis. Day or night, it's magic.

FREE ADMISSION DAYS

You can also visit the Acropolis for free on certain days of the year. This also applies to the National Archaeological Museum, the Roman Agora and other government-run museums and archaeological sites, but not private museums.

The dates are:

- Sundays from 1 November and 31 March
- The first Sunday of April, May, June and October (unless the first Sunday is a holiday, when the second Sunday is free)
- National holidays
- 6 March (in memory of Melina Mercouri)
- 18 April (International Monuments Day)
- 18 May (International Museums Day)
- 5 June (International Environment Day)
- The last weekend of September (European Heritage Days)

When it rains

This is not likely to be a problem in the summer months, but it does rain in Athens, so it's as well to have some ideas of what to do if it happens. Fortunately Athens has plenty of museums, and in some ways you can regard rain as a blessing – being indoors in the sunshine can be frustrating!

If it rained from dawn till dusk, you could probably spend all that time in the National Archaeological Museum and not get bored. Most people would probably prefer a little variety, though, in which case there are two areas to head for in a downpour. One is the Plaka, where as well as sheltering in shops there are also several museums to explore, including the Museum of Greek Folk Art, Museum of Greek Musical Instruments, the Kanellopoulos Museum, the Jewish Museum, the Ceramics Museum and also several churches, including the new and old cathedrals. Otherwise make for Vassilissis Sofias, the main street which runs from Syntagma Square past the north side of the Parliament building. Here you'll find in close proximity the Benaki Museum, the Museum of Cycladic Art, the Byzantine Museum, the War Museum and the National Gallery, which should provide something for everyone.

If you prefer couture to culture, the shops in the Kolonaki district, immediately north of Vassilissis Sofias, will keep you occupied. For more basic high-street shopping, the pedestrianised Ermou will keep you both out of the traffic and out of the rain, though not necessarily out of debt. If you don't trust yourself to keep control of your credit card, a cheaper option to keep you dry is to visit one of the city's numerous cinemas (see page 31).

◐ *The National Archaeological Museum is easily worth a full day's visit*

On arrival

TIME DIFFERENCES

Athens is on East European Time (EET). During Daylight Savings Time, which in Greece begins at 02.00 on the last Sunday in March and ends at 02.00 on the last Sunday in October, the clocks go forward 1 hour. When it is noon in the summertime in Athens, time at home is:

Australia Eastern Standard Time 19.00, Central Standard Time 18.30, Western Standard Time 17.00.

New Zealand 21.00.

South Africa 11.00.

UK and Republic of Ireland 10.00.

USA and Canada Newfoundland Time 06.30, Atlantic Canada Time 06.00, Eastern Time 05.00, Central Time 04.00, Mountain Time 03.00, Pacific Time 02.00, Alaska 01.00.

ARRIVING

By air

Athens International Airport is known as Eleftherios Venizelos and is 27 km (17 miles) north-east of the city centre and linked to Athens by a 6-lane highway, metro, buses and taxis. It is an excellent, modern airport that has all the facilities you would expect, including a tourist information office, ATMs, 24-hour luggage storage, restaurants, cafés, shops and car hire offices.

The easiest way into the city is using metro line 3, which has two trains an hour (🕑 06.00–24.00) and takes about 30 minutes to Syntagma Square; single fare is €6. The Express Bus number E95 runs 2–4 times per hour, depending on the time of day, and should also take about 30 minutes into Syntagma, but can be slower if the

◔ Athens' Eleftherios Venizelos Airport is well connected to the city and suburbs

traffic is busy. The fare is €2.90. There are other services, including the E96 to Pireas and the E92 to Kifissia, though these are slightly less frequent. Buses run 24 hours. Taxis take about 25–30 minutes when traffic is light, but can be up to an hour in the rush hour. The fare should be about €15 during the day but can be up to €30 at night. Make sure the meter is switched on, or agree a flat fee beforehand. If using the meter, note that there are additional and legitimate charges for the transport of luggage, for late-night journeys and for going to and from the airport.

Athens International Airport ☎ 210 353 000. ⓦ www.aia.gr
Tourist office ☎ 210 354 5101. ⏱ Mon–Fri 09.00–19.00, Sat & Sun 10.00–15.00.

By ferry

Ferries dock at the main port, Pireas, which is linked to the city centre by metro (⏱ 06.00–24.00). Otherwise take a taxi, which should be no more than about €10 to the centre of Athens.

By rail

International arrivals come in at the Larissa station, as do trains from northern parts of Greece, while trains from the Peloponnese region of Greece arrive at the nearby Peloponnisou station. Both are to the north-west of the city centre and have metro, bus, tram and taxi links. The suburb they are in is one of the poorer parts of Athens, so take care of your bags and do not get involved with anyone offering you help or cheap hotel rooms.

Larissa Station ⓐ Deliyianni 31. ☎ 210 529 7777. ⏱ Daily 06.30–24.00. Ⓜ Metro: Larissa station
Peloponnisou Station ⓐ Sidirodromon. ☎ 210 513 1601. ⏱ Daily 06.30–24.00. Ⓜ Metro: Larissa station.

Driving

The best advice is: don't. Driving in Athens is a nightmare, even for those experienced in driving in Greece and in other European capitals. The traffic is heavy, signposting is poor, and you need to have a good mental map of the city, as well as a real one, in order to navigate your way around. If you really have no option but to drive into Athens, try to plan your route in advance as much as you can, and take it slowly.

Parking in Athens makes driving look like the easy part. There are no parking meters, and only a handful of not-well-signposted official car parks. There are quite a few unofficial car parks, on vacant lots, and your best bet is to park wherever you can, and pay up. Local drivers pay little regard to official, or unofficial, parking rules. They may park on the pavement, block another car in (be prepared for this to happen to you) and be prepared to get a ticket from the police if necessary.

FINDING YOUR FEET

Athens is easy to get to grips with, once you're accustomed to the volume of traffic and the unexpectedly fast pace of life in what is a laid-back nation. Drivers have little regard for pedestrians, so if

STREETS AHEAD

The Greek word for a street is *Odos*. Apart from the occasional Avenue (*Leoforos*), almost every address in the country is on a street. For that reason, the word *Odos* is seldom used when giving an address, and you will usually see just a single name. Odos Adrianou is simply Adrianou. Street numbers are usually given after the name, so the address of the Agora, for example, is Adrianou 24.

IF YOU GET LOST, TRY ...

Excuse me, do you speak English?
Με συγχωρείτε, μήπως μιλάτε Αγγλικά;
Me sinhorite, mipos milate Anglika?

Excuse me, is this the right way to the city centre/the tourist office/the station?
Με συγχωρείτε μπορείτε να μου πείτε πώς θα πάω το κέντρο της πόλεως/τουριστικό γραφείο πληροφοριών/ σιδηροδρομικό σταθμό;
Me sinhorite, borite na mu pite pos tha pao to kentro tis poleos/turistiko grafio pliroforion/sidirodromiko stathmo?

Can you point to it on my map?
Μπορείτε να μου το υποδείξετε στο χάρτη;
Borite na mu to ipodixete sto harti?

crossing a busy street you should stick to the official crossings, look in every direction and cross when other people cross.

Athens is one of the safest cities in the world, with a comparatively low crime rate, but there are still petty thieves and pickpockets about, so take care of your belongings. The city centre, where most visitors are likely to spend time, is pretty safe till late at night, but like anywhere else, don't walk alone down dark alleys. Of the areas covered by this book, the streets around Omonia Square are where you probably need to be most on your guard, especially late at night. That said, few visitors have any problems at all.

Έξοδος
Exit

● *The modern metro system makes getting around Athens easy*

Railway stations

Omonia Square

Konstandinoupoleos

Pireos

Athinas

Gazi

Keramikos

PSYRRI

Ermou

Monastiraki

Erm

Theseum

Mitropol

AGORA

Roman Forum

PLAKA

Parthenon

ACROPOLIS

Dora Stratou Theatre

FILOPAPPOU

Airport

Theatre

LYKAVITTOS

St George's

Eleftherias
Park

Akadimias

zelou

Vassilissis Sofias

KOLONAKI

Vassilissis Sofias

Vassilissis Sofias

ntagma
Square

Parliament
Building

National Garden

Vassileos Konstantinou

Presidential
Palace

Armaïas

Zappeion

Stadiou
Square

Panathenaic
Stadium

N

0   500m

ORIENTATION

Finding your way around Athens is relatively easy, once you have a few landmarks and streets in your head. There are several long, straight streets which connect the main squares, and if you get lost you should eventually come out on one of them.

The main squares are Syntagma and Omonia. With the smaller square of Monastiraki, these form a convenient triangle for orientation. Ermou links Monastiraki with Syntagma, Stadiou runs from Syntagma to Omonia, and Athinas runs from Omonia to Monastiraki. South of Monastiraki is the Acropolis, and north-east of Syntagma is Lykavittos Hill: these two high points can be seen from several parts of the city, and are also useful navigation tools.

GETTING AROUND

You can get round central Athens easily on foot. Most of the main sights you would want to see are in the centre, and walking is the easiest option. It shouldn't take more than 30–40 minutes to walk from one side of the city centre to the other.

Buses & trams

You shouldn't need to use these except when going out of the city centre. They are cheap and have a good network, but can also be crowded. You must buy your ticket before travelling from the OASA (Athens Transport Organisation) ticket booth which is near every stop. Drivers do not issue tickets and you must validate your ticket by inserting it into the stamping machine when you get on the bus. Reaching the machine in a crowded bus is another matter.

Metro

The metro network is not extensive, with only three lines, but is

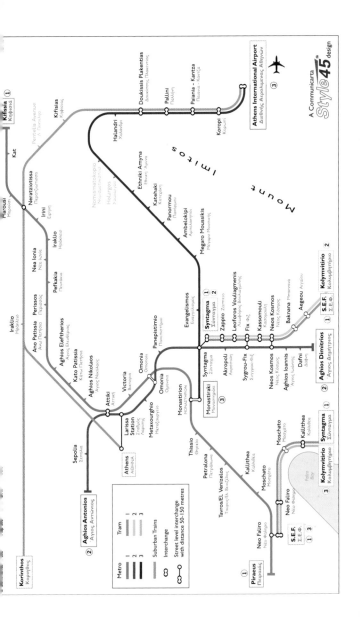

efficient. Trains run every 5 minutes during the rush hours, every 10 minutes at other times and the service operates 05.30–24.00. Look for the large M signs, indicating the stations. There are ticket offices and ticket machines inside the stations, and you must validate your ticket when entering. It then remains valid for 90 minutes or for one journey (which can involve changes but not a return along the same line). A ticket for Line 1 is €0.60, and for Lines 2 and 3 (or combining 2 and 3 with Line 1) is €0.70.

Taxis

Taxis are widespread and not expensive. Everyone in Athens uses them, which can make them hard to find at peak periods. Just wave one down in the street, and be prepared for the local practice of cab-sharing. A driver is legally entitled to take more than one passenger if all are going in the same direction, and charge the full fare for each. The meter shows either Tariff 1 or Tariff 2. The first operates from 05.00 to 24.00 and within the city limits. Tariff 2 applies overnight or if going outside the city limits. If you feel you are being cheated, ask the driver to find a policeman to check the fare.

CAR HIRE

You don't need a car if staying in Athens, but if you do want to hire one it is probably better to do it in advance. Collecting from and returning to the airport is the best option, if you can, to avoid the city centre traffic. Most hotels will help with car hire, and the major international companies, and several exclusively Greek ones, all have offices in the city centre.

● *Take the funicular up Lykavittos hill for bird's-eye views*

THE CITY OF
Athens

Around the Acropolis

Just as Syntagma Square and the Greek Parliament building is the centre of modern Athens, so was the Acropolis the centre of the ancient city. It was on the slopes of this natural hill that the first city inhabitants began to live, long before the Parthenon temple was built on the top. Today the Parthenon still stands, looking out over the city and visible from much of the centre.

The shorter your visit, the more time you are likely to spend in this area. The Acropolis itself should be everyone's first port of call, and most visitors then explore the streets of the Plaka district on its northern side. Once you find your way round here, the Parthenon becomes a good focal point to help you navigate your way round the rest of the city. The area is full of eating places, bars, cafés, museums, archaeological sites and you could spend a week here and not get bored.

SIGHTS & ATTRACTIONS

The Acropolis

The Acropolis, topped by the symmetrical perfection of the Parthenon temple, is not merely the greatest monument in the city, it is one of the greatest in the world. Even return visitors find themselves drawn back to it, as it is so full of history – a history you can really feel as you explore the top of this rocky hill around which the city was founded.

The word acropolis means 'upper city', and there are many of these scattered all over Greece, but none has the grace and majesty of the one in Athens. Its crowning glory is the Parthenon temple, but there are several more buildings around it, all of them built in the

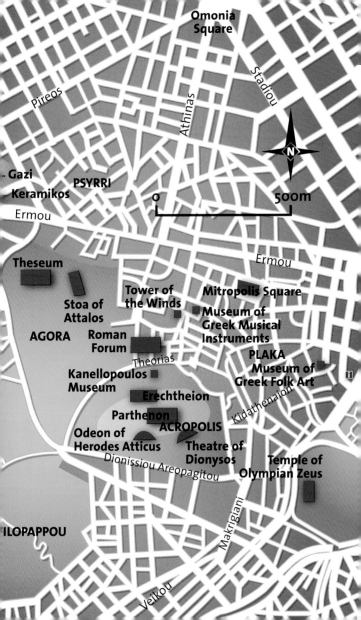

5th century BC during the city's so-called Golden Age. The greatest sculptor of the day, Pheidias, oversaw the building work up here. The finest marble was brought from quarries outside the city, and the best craftsmen employed to turn the pieces into a beautifully proportioned whole. No straight lines were used in its construction. Even the steps were very gently curved to create something which appears to be straight yet is more pleasing to the eye.

After admiring the Parthenon, take time to examine the other buildings, which include the smaller Temple of Athena Nike. There is also a museum here, at the far end of the hilltop from the entrance and well worth a visit. Allow at least an hour up here – one of the world's finest buildings deserves nothing less.

🛈 (site) 210 321 0219; (museum) 210 323 6665. 🕑 Daily. Apr–Dec

🔽 *The Acropolis was the centre and citadel of ancient Athens*

08.00–sunset (museum opens 10.00 on Mon); Jan–Mar 08.30–14.30 (museum opens 11.00 on Mon)

Theatre of Dionysos

Dating back to the 6th century BC, this venerable theatre could hold 17,000 spectators in 64 rows of seats. It was used by the Romans for gladiator contests and wild animal fights, and had been used by the ancient Greeks during the Golden Age of Athens for the city's annual Drama Festival. It was on this spot, then, that modern European drama was born, and the works of authors such as Sophocles and Aristophanes had their first performances here.

🅐 Leoforos Dionysiou Areopagitou. 🏛 210 322 4625. 🕐 Daily. May–Oct 08.30–19.00; Nov–Apr 08.00–sunset.

Odeon of Herodes Atticus

Looking down from the southern side of the Acropolis you can see this splendid ancient theatre, which was built in AD161–174 by a wealthy businessman from Marathon, Tiberius Claudius Atticus Herodes, and sympathetically restored in the years following World War II. It can seat 5000 people and has been used as the main setting for music, dance and dramas during the Athens Festival (see page 9) ever since 1955. The Odeon is otherwise closed to visitors.
③ Leoforos Dionysiou Areopagitou.

Temple of Olympian Zeus

This massive temple, also known as the Olympieion, dates back originally to the 6th century BC. Several attempts were made to complete it, but it wasn't finished until the Emperor Hadrian did the job in AD130. It was then the biggest temple in Greece, bigger than the Parthenon and the temple at Delphi. Even though only 15 columns now remain standing, they give a very good impression of how monumental it must have been. The columns are about 17 m (56 ft) high and originally there were 104 of them. The bases of some and remnants of others lie around, and one complete column has been left where it fell in 1852.
③ Leoforos Olgas 1. **①** 210 922 6330. **◐** Daily 08.30–15.00.

The Plaka

The Plaka district, on the northern slopes of the Acropolis, has been a magnet for visitors for years. It can seem to be very much a tourist trap, but you will also see Athenians strolling its streets, along with Greek holidaymakers spending a few days in the capital, and other

◐ *Surviving fragments of the Temple of Olympian Zeus give an idea of its original scale*

visitors from all over the world. It's an attractive district with many elegant buildings dating back to the 19th century, when it was redeveloped. Many of these are now housing souvenir shops on their lower floors, but others have been preserved and some are used as museums.

Aside from the museums (see under 'Culture' on pages 68–71 for the major ones), the area is also popular for eating and drinking, though you need to take a little care over where you choose. Many of the places on the main streets cater to tourists, who are here today and gone tomorrow and not likely to return whether they get a good meal or not.

The Agora

The Agora, or marketplace of ancient Athens, is the best archaeological site in the city after the Acropolis. After wandering round the Parthenon on top of the Acropolis, it's fascinating to walk down the hill and enter the remains of the Agora. There is still enough here by way of foundations and layout for you to people the place in your mind with stallholders and shoppers, to imagine them going about their business and gossiping about events in the city. It became a marketplace in the 6th century BC (before that it had been a cemetery), and remained the hub of ordinary Athenian life for several centuries.

At one end of the site is the beautiful little Temple of Hephaistos. This is one of the best-preserved temples in Greece, and is very significant as it was the building of this temple in 449–444BC which marked the start of the Golden Age of Athens under Pericles. At the other side of the Agora is another impressive building, the Stoa of Attalos. This two-storey building with its colonnades was constructed in the 2nd century BC, and has been beautifully restored by the American School of Archaeology. It's the only chance you will get to see a building from that era as it would have looked at the time, and it now houses a small but fascinating museum.

ⓐ Adrianou 24. ⓘ 210 321 0185. ⓛ Daily. May–Oct 08.00–19.00; Nov–Apr 08.00–17.00.

The Roman Forum

The Roman counterpart of the nearby Agora has few items of specific interest other than its gateway and the picturesque Tower of the Winds, an octagonal building of the 1st century AD, which originally housed a water-clock for the convenience of ancient shoppers in the Forum.

Mitropolis Square

Athens has two cathedrals, side by side in Mitropolis Square, and they could hardly be more different. The square is dominated by the large modern Great Mitropolis Cathedral, which was built in 1842–62 on the site of a monastery that had been destroyed in 1827. The interior is cavernous and has a rather grand and serious feel, and the building is usually open daily from dawn until dusk. The smaller building next door to it is easily missed, but is far more atmospheric. This is the picturesque 12th-century Little Mitropolis, only 11 m (36 ft) long. It isn't always open, but you should definitely go in if it is, to see its tiny interior with the candles burning inside.

ⓐ Plateia Mitropoleos

Keramikos Cemetery

This was the main cemetery for ancient Athens, and many of the tombs still survive in a green oasis of peace beside the busy Ermou road. The name comes from Ancient Greek *keramos*, pottery (hence also our word 'ceramics'): this was the part of the city where the potters could all be found. Apart from the fascinating tombs with their inscriptions, some of which have been dated back to the 12th century BC, the site also has a small museum containing some of the more unusual finds. Some of the gravestones uncovered when the site was excavated in the 1930s are incredibly moving, the grief on them passing down the centuries. Keramikos is also a good site for the city's wildlife. There are terrapins and lizards in the grass, and numerous birds flit through the olive trees. If not for the traffic noise, the people here would still be resting in peace over 3000 years after they were buried.

🅰 Ermou 148. ☎ 210 346 3552. 🕒 Daily. Apr–Sep 08.00–10.00; Oct–Mar 08.30–15.00.

CULTURE

Kanellopoulos Museum

This museum is housed in a neo-classical Plaka mansion that was built in 1884. It's a large collection of ancient artefacts that was originally owned by Paul and Alexandra Kanellopoulos. Like many collections that have been acquired by individuals over many years, it is eclectic yet shows an eye for items that are both beautiful and quirky. There are erotic carvings and religious icons almost side by side. Some cases contain exquisite jewellery, others have ceramics. There are tiny ornate pins from Persia and also a huge block of stone which one day fell off the Acropolis. The rooms are spacious and light, and the collection well-labelled in both English and Greek.

🅰 Panos/Theorias. ☎ 210 321 2313. 🕒 Tue–Sun 08.30–15.00.

▶ *Keramikos, 'Potter's Field', has a poignant beauty*

Museum of Greek Musical Instruments

This is one of the best small museums in Athens, also housed in a Plaka mansion, this one built in 1842. What could be a dull if worthy subject is here made lots of fun because you can listen to the sounds of the different instruments using free headphones that are provided at most of the cases. It's fascinating to hear these sometimes historic recordings while admiring the skill and ingenuity with which some of these instruments were made. They include not just the familiar bouzouki and guitar but also lyres, bagpipes, shepherds' pipes and even bells worn by livestock.

○ *Listen to the sounds and admire the workmanship*

🅰 Diogenous 1–3. ☎ 210 325 0198/4119. 🕐 Tue & Thu–Sun 10.00–15.00, Wed 12.00–18.00.

Museum of Greek Folk Art

Another excellent Plaka museum. It's a large collection on five floors of another old mansion, and can become very absorbing, so if you have an interest in the subject, allow at least an hour or so for a visit. It's fascinating to see examples of work from the different Greek islands, and from parts of the mainland which are less familiar to the average visitor. There is a large collection of beautiful embroidery, and another of traditional costumes including those used in folk dances, such as the rather scary-looking Skyros Goat Dance. There's fine jewellery too, paintings, religious items, domestic objects and also changing exhibitions. These are often photographic displays, and can be very impressive. The museum also has a small shop on the ground floor which sells books, postcards and craft items.

🅰 Kidathinaion 17. ☎ 210 321 3018/322 9031. 🕐 Tue–Sun 10.00–14.00.

RETAIL THERAPY

The Plaka's two busiest streets, Kidathinaion and Adrianou, are lined with souvenir shops, and do look inside as some of them are huge and stock a good range of quality items like ceramics and jewellery. The streets west of Monastiraki Square form the bazaar area, at its busiest on Sunday mornings when the street market arrives, but there's a smaller market on Saturdays and shops are open all week. **Centre of Hellenic Tradition** is a great place to find Greek arts and crafts, both old and new. 🅰 In the arcade between Metropoleos 59 and Pandrossou 36.

TAKING A BREAK

Eden €€ When Athens' first vegetarian restaurant opened several years ago, it was thought of as a bit of a gimmick, but now the Eden is established as one of the best places in town. Non-vegetarians happily eat here, the food is wonderfully tasty, and your coffee cup is happily replenished, American-style. It's the perfect place to call in for a lunch, dinner, snack, coffee or a glass of wine.
ⓐ Lissiou 12. ① 210 324 8858. ① Wed–Mon 11.00–24.00.

AFTER DARK

Psyrri

For many years the Psyrri district was a rather run-down area of the city centre, filled with half-derelict buildings and grubby factories. It has since been transformed into one of the most happening areas of Athens, as empty buildings have turned into bars, and workshops into ouzeries. It's now one of the main nightlife centres, where younger Athenians often go to avoid the tourist traps in the Plaka district. It's right next door to the Plaka too, on the other side of Ermou and roughly in the triangle of streets bordered by Ermou, Athinas and Pireas. It's a great place to wander round from the early evening onwards, with restaurants ranging from funky to fine-dining, alongside music bars and cafés. You'll want to see the Plaka, but you'll want to eat and drink in the Psyrri and just beyond the Gazi district – the new Psyrri.

Restaurants

Bakalarakia € One of the Plaka's basic basement tavernas, much older and more reliable than many of the smart places on the street. This is named after its speciality, a cod dish served with a garlic sauce.

🅐 Kidathineon 41. 🕿 210 322 5084. 🕐 Mon–Sat 18.00–23.00. Closed Aug.

O Platanos € It sometimes seems as if 'The Plane Tree' has been here for as long as the Acropolis, so well established is it in its leafy square. Visitors love it but locals hang out here too, and though the food is nothing fancy, it is wonderfully cooked. Great atmosphere too, whether outside or inside.

🅐 Diogenous 4. 🕿 210 322 0666. 🕐 Daily 11.00–15.00, 18.00–23.00. Closed Aug.

To Kouti €€ One of the few reliable places on this busy Plaka street, most of the others catering for the fast tourist trade. Here the service is more leisurely, the menu's unusual and the setting with its Acropolis views will give you a romantic night to remember.

🅐 Adrianou 23. 🕿 210 321 3229. 🕐 Daily 13.00–01.00.

Edodi €€€ With just eight tables, you'll need to book ahead to sample some of the best cooking in Athens. The food is displayed at your table before it's cooked, so you know it's fresh and what the chef proposes to do with it. An expensive indulgence.

🅐 Veikou 80. 🕿 210 921 3013. 🕐 Mon–Sat 20.00–00.30. Closed Aug.

Spondi €€€ Athens, too, now has its Michelin stars, a thought that would have been ludicrous not so long ago. This neo-classical mansion has contemporary art on the walls and has been voted the best restaurant in Greece four years in a row.

🅐 Pyrronos 5, Varnava Square. 🕿 210 752 4021. 🕐 Daily 20.00–13.00.

Omonia

Omonia is the city's second major square but has always been rather down-at-heel compared to the smarter Syntagma. It's been like the disreputable brother, who has his charms but they're sometimes hard to see. Omonia has always had roads and traffic coming into it from all directions, making it noisy and difficult to cross. Its proximity to the Central Market has also meant that it has always been a very dubious area, as city market areas tend to be, attracting casual workers, immigrants, people on the edges of society. For that reason you still should not linger there after dark, and even during the day keep an eye on your possessions. During the day it is always crowded, and you're not likely to be mugged down a quiet street, but watch out for pickpockets taking advantage of the crowds.

That said, Omonia is improving, just as the whole of Athens has been smartened up in recent years. Olive trees have been planted in the centre of the square, and you have a wonderful view straight down Athinas towards the Acropolis. New smart hotels and eating places have started to open around Omonia, and the buildings which face on to the square have been given a good clean and facelift, in the hope that the Omonia area will be regenerated, as happened to the Psyrri and Gazi districts to the south-west. From the south-east corner of Omonia one of the city's main thoroughfares, Stadiou, leads in a straight line to Syntagma. From the eastern side of the square another major street, Venizelou (also called Panepistimiou), also leads to Syntagma, after a dog-leg at the start. The streets leading off Omonia can be confusing as there are so many of them and some go at angles and cross each other. If you leave Omonia at its north-east corner and head along 28 Oktovriou

National
Archaeological
Museum

Exarhia
District &
Polytechnic

Marni

Marni

Marni

28Oktovriou/Patission

Kaningos

Omonia
Square

Em. Benaki

Pireos

Venizelou/Panepistimiou

City Hall

Sofokleous

Stadiou

Theatrou
Square   Theatrou

Athinas

Central
Market

Museum of
the City of Athens

N

0   500m

Ermou

Mitropoli
Square

(28th October Street, also called Patission) you will come after a few blocks to the National Archaeological Museum, the city's other unmissable focus alongside the Acropolis.

SIGHTS & ATTRACTONS

Omonia Square

Omonia Square (Platia Omonias) used to be a very attractive square, with fountains, bushes and benches, but this was before the car was king and traffic hemmed in the little platia on all sides. Then for many years there was a permanent display of iron and wooden hoardings, behind which the noise of drills and hammers added to the cacophony. In the nearby streets you would see painters and decorators waiting by the road, looking for casual hire, and immigrants would be selling cheap cigarettes. At night it became the red-light district. In other words it had much more of a rough Balkan feel to it than the smart western European ambitions of Syntagma.

All of this is still there, if perhaps in a slightly watered-down version these days as the area starts to smarten itself up. Olive trees, the old symbol of the city, have been planted in the centre, and there is talk of pedestrianising Athinas. This would allow locals and visitors alike to stroll all the way down to Monastiraki Square while gazing towards the Acropolis, without taking their life in their hands in the traffic.

Omonia is one of the main metro hubs, where Line 1 from Kifissia to Pireas intersects with Line 2, which runs from north-west to south-east across the city and which is still being extended. Up

▶ *The olive trees are back in Omonia Square*

above ground Omonia is the place to head for if you want to buy international newspapers and magazines from the constantly busy kiosks, cheap watches or leather belts from the roadside vendors (no, it isn't a real Gucci or Rolex), eat fast food or dine in one of the more interesting old restaurants that can also be searched out here – see the same recommendations later in this chapter. But love it or hate it, Omonia is Omonia, an essential part of the mosaic that is Athens.

Central Market

Walk a few blocks south from Omonia down Athinas and you come to the Central Market. Whereas in cities like London and Paris the

⬤ *Central Market is where you make contact with the real everyday Athens*

old city markets have been dug up and sent to the suburbs, the sites turned into shopping centres, here in Athens the market is still thriving. With the loss of Covent Garden and Les Halles, something gutsy (literally) went out of the lives of those cities, but in Athens the market heart still beats. That's partly because it is a market for shoppers as well as for the trade and you're as likely to find a housewife buying a chicken as a restaurateur examining the squid and the octopus.

There is a main market building which vegetarians may prefer not to enter, as stall after stall is laid out with every animal and cut of meat the earth can provide and everything familiar and unfamiliar from beneath the waves. Naturally there are also what seem to be millions of olives of all kinds, and nuts and cheeses galore. But it's not just in the main hall, as the streets around are filled with shops which also sell local produce.

ⓐ Athinas

CULTURE

National Archaeological Museum

This is, without argument, one of the finest museums in the world, and no visit to the city would be complete without seeing it. What makes it special is that, unlike many museums (the British Museum, for example), it displays mainly the treasures of one civilisation, Greece, though a new wing contains a collection of Egyptian items showing how that culture influenced Greek artists. And what Greek treasures there are. You should allow at least half a day for a visit, although like many visitors you might get museum fatigue and want to make a couple of shorter visits. To get the most out of it you should at the very least buy one of the official museum guidebooks, or you could also take an audio tour or hire one of the official museum guides, who offer tours in several languages.

If time is really precious, there are certain objects you really must see. Among these are the wonderful treasures unearthed at Mycenae by Heinrich Schliemann (see page 138), in particular the golden mask which was thought to show the face of Agamemnon. Some of the other highlights are hard to miss as they are displayed in places which draw attention to them. The massive statue of the God Poseidon about to throw his trident is one of these, as is the equally powerful bronze piece showing a boy riding a horse and known as 'The Jockey-Boy'. In fact both these important works were taken together from the sea off the coast of Evia in 1927.

The National Archaeological Museum is a must-see destination

Up the stairs is a stunning collection of frescoes from the island of Santorini (Thira). These were immaculately preserved in the huge volcanic eruption that happened in the 16th century BC, and must not be missed. The beautiful colour and detail is breathtaking, bringing the world, the people and the artists alive before your eyes. There have been discussions about moving these back to Santorini for display there, but they look set to stay in Athens for the moment. And these are but a tiny few of the thousands of fabulous items in this impressive museum.

ⓐ Patission 44. ⓣ 210 821 7717. ⓛ Apr–Oct, Tue–Sun 08.00–19.00, Mon 12.00–19.00; Nov–Mar, Tue–Sun 08.30–15.00.

Museum of the City of Athens

Though only a small museum, it's worth a visit to see the collection of paintings of Athens over the years, including work by Turner and Edward Lear, and a wonderfully detailed scale model of the small town which Athens was in 1842. That was the year that Greece's first King, Otto of Bavaria, moved out of this house and into his new palace, now the Parliament Building. Many of the rooms here are done out as they would have looked during the six years that Otto lived here.

ⓐ Paparigopolou 7. ⓣ 210 324 6164. ⓛ Thu–Tue 10.30–18.00, Wed 12.00–20.00.

RETAIL THERAPY

If you're impressed by the contents of the National Archaeological Museum, then its shop just inside the entrance has a fine collection of museum reproductions (though note that it is closed on Sundays).

The area around the Central Market is great for foodies. You might not be able to take home a leg of lamb, but there are plenty of more easily transportable items, such as honey, wines and spirits, olives, herbs and spices, cooking and serving utensils, kitchen gadgets and many more besides. It's also a great place to come if you're planning a picnic for a day out – grab some bread, olives, cheese and tomatoes, and perhaps some halva for dessert.

AFTER DARK

Restaurants

Athinaikon € Wonderful, venerable place with its wooden interior still intact, and some of the waiters dating from the same era. They have one of the best *meze* menus in town, dozens of dishes made fresh every day so it's a chance to try lots of different things like grilled octopus or deep-fried whitebait. ❸ Themistokleous 2. ❶ 210 383 8485. ❶ Mon–Sat 11.30–00.30. Closed Aug.

Barba Yannis € You won't regret a night out at Barba Yannis – if you can get in, because when it's busy they queue outside, though there are some tables outside in summer too. It's the kind of place where everyone seems to know everyone, there's always a buzz and the food is simple but excellent, mostly meaty oven dishes. ❸ Emmanuel Benaki 94. ❶ 210 330 0185. ❶ Mon–Sat 12.00–late, Sun 12.00–15.00. Closed Aug.

Diporto € If you want a real Athens eating experience then head for this old place in a basement beneath the Central Market, where the market traders go for good, honest, fresh, hearty food, though you'll find local businesspeople there too. If you're on a budget, it's ideal.

There's no phone. ⓐ Corner of Theatrou and Sokratous. ⏱ Mon–Sat 12.00–18.00.

Ideal €–€€ Smart but friendly city centre institution where you will get the finest examples of Greek staples such as *stifado* and moussaka. ⓐ Panepistimiou 46. ☎ 210 330 3000. ⏱ Mon–Sat 11.00–15.00, 18.00–23.00.

Entertainment

As with all edgy districts, this is where some of the best nightlife is. As long as you take obvious precautions, you'll be safer here at night than in most cities in Europe. But don't go wandering round alone if you've had too much to drink, and that goes double for female visitors. That said, you'll be in the company of lots of Athenians, all come to have a good time – and Athenians are past masters at doing that. Head for the Exarhia district, which is behind the National Archaeological Museum and close to the Polytechnic: find students and you'll find the good nightlife. Alternatively the areas around Omonia, and south-west from Omonia along Pireas, are also good entertainment districts.

After Dark This is just one of the bars in Exarhia where you'll hear eclectic music and rub shoulders with the local students and artsy crowd. ⓐ Diodotou 31. ☎ 210 360 6460. ⏱ Nightly 21.30–late.

Stoa Athanaton Off Athinas to the north of the Central Market is this old taverna, where you'll also get live bouzouki music in the evenings – late in the evenings, that is, because if you look at the opening hours you'll realise this is no conventional taverna. ⓐ Sofokleous 19. ☎ 210 321 4362. ⏱ Mon–Sat 15.00–18.00, 00.00–06.00 Sept–Apr.

Syntagma

Syntagma Square is the centre of the modern Greek city. At the top
is the Greek Parliament building, and it is in this square that
Athenians will gather whenever they wish to make their voice
heard. By the side of the Parliament and leading off Syntagma is
Vasilissis Sofias. This street has several excellent museums along it,
and to the north of it is the area of Kolonaki, one of the more
expensive and exclusive of the inner-city districts. North of Kolonaki
is Lykavittos Hill, a clear landmark just as the Acropolis is further
south. To the south-east of Syntagma are the National Gardens, a
welcome bit of shade and greenery right in the city centre. Across
the street from the southern end of the National Gardens is the
Panathenaic Stadium, where the 1896 Olympic Games were held
and are still in use today. There are few really ancient sites in this
area, at least on the surface. Building of the fairly new Syntagma
metro station was held up several times when archaeological
remains were found during excavation. No matter how new the city
centre appears to be, a few feet below the streets and pavement,
thousands of years of history are hidden.

SIGHTS & ATTRACTIONS

Syntagma Square
Constitution Square, the English name of Syntagma (also spelt
Syndagma or Sindagma), tells you that this is the political heart of
Athens. Look to the east and the grand neo-classical Parliament
Building (or Vouli) stands at the top of the square. In front of this is
where the Changing of the Guard ceremony takes place (see page
44), and where the Tomb of the Unknown Soldier lies. Syntagma is a

Theatre

LYKAVITTOS

St George's

Funicular

Platia Mavili

Pl. Dexameni

Ploutarchou

Haritos

Pindarou

Tsakalof

KOLONAKI

Karneadou

Benaki
Museum

Vassilissis Sofias

Vassilissis Sofias

Vassilissis Sofias

ntagma
uare

Parliament
Building

Goulandris
Museum

Byzantine
Museum

War
Museum

National
Gallery

National Garden

Presidential
Palace

Vassileos Konstantinou

N

Zappeion

0

500m

Panathenaic
Stadium

large and fairly open square, transformed since the new metro station opened there. A fountain plays in the centre of the square, there's plenty of greenery around, and benches to sit on. Although many of the surrounding buildings are office buildings, there are also a few cafés, kiosks selling international newspapers and a general air of relaxed bustle.

On one side of the square is the Grande Bretagne Hotel, almost as much a landmark as the Parliament itself. It was built in 1862 as an annex to the Parliament Building, which at that time was the summer palace for the Greek royal family. Guests have included Sir Winston Churchill and Elizabeth Taylor – though not together. Churchill stayed during World War II, and an attempt was made on his life while he was there. It's worth going into the hotel lobby just to take a look, even if you're not staying there.

Parliament Building

This elegant building has had a chequered history, housing everyone from royalty to the homeless, and today it's where the Greek Parliament sits. It was built in 1842 as the summer palace for the first Greek king, Otto of Bavaria. It was used less and less over the years, and in the 1920s when several hundred thousand Christian Greeks came to Athens, having been expelled from Muslim Turkey, the building was used to house many of them. It was renovated in 1926 and opened as the home of the Greek Parliament. It is not open to the public.

Presidential Palace

To the east of the National Gardens and a stone's throw from the

▶ *The Parliament Building dominates Syntagma*

Parliament Building is the Presidential Palace. Little wonder that the Greeks had a sceptical attitude to the monarchy, when this grand neo-classical royal home was but a few hundred yards from their summer palace, which in turn had an annexe built onto it, now the Grand Bretagne hotel (see page 86). Built in 1878, it was a royal home till the exile of King Constantine in 1967 when the Colonels came to power.

Although it is not open to the public it too is protected by the Greek soldiers (*Evzones*) in their traditional uniforms and worth seeing for this reason. You can only get a glimpse of the attractive-looking gardens over the wall.

❸ Irodou Attikou.

National Garden and Zappeion

Right next to the bustle of Syntagma Square, and the boisterous debates in the Parliament building, is the oasis of calm that is the National Garden. This is the city's only major park, and it provides citizens with peace and shade, as they pause to read a newspaper or take children in there to play, away from the traffic.

The garden was originally laid out in the 1840s by Queen Amalia, when the Parliament was the Royal Palace, for the private use of the royal family. Today it's for everyone to enjoy, and the 16 hectares (39¹/₂ acres) includes some quite lush greenery, ponds with terrapins and fish, a small and not too attractive zoo, a botanical museum and a children's playground.

The only major building within the Garden is towards the southern end, where there is also a café. That is the Zappeion Exhibition Hall, an imposingly graceful late 19th-century building which is now used as a conference centre.

Panathenaic Stadium (Olympic Stadium of 1896)

Across the road from the National Gardens, at the south-east corner, is one of the city centre's loveliest attractions, the Stadio, or Olympic Stadium. As you gaze at the graceful lines of the curved stone seating, imagine that on this site in the 4th century BC the precursors of the Olympic Games, the Panathenaic Games, were being held. Look across to the Acropolis and you really appreciate the history of this unique city.

The original Panathenaic Stadium has long disappeared, and in its place the Stadio was built for the first modern Olympic Games, held in 1896. The stadium was built to the same design as the original, which was described by Pausanias in the 2nd century AD. It has the same 47 rows of seats, with room for 60,000 spectators around three sides of the stadium, the fourth side left open to look out at the city. In the middle is a running track, where you might see joggers exercising, and it's still in use competitively too, since the annual Athens Marathon finishes here, as did the Marathon in the 2004 Olympics, when the Games came back to their homeland again.

🅐 Leoforos Ardhittou. 🕐 Daily sunrise–sunset.

Lykavittos

The city's second great visual landmark after the Acropolis, and equally useful for getting your bearings, is Lykavittos Hill (also called Lykabettos.) At 278 m (912 ft) it's the highest hill in the city, and naturally popular for its views, especially in the evening when Athens is lit up and you can look across to the illuminated Parthenon on top of the Acropolis. The easy way up, and popular with children, is the funicular. You can find this at the top of Ploutarchou, and its operating hours vary so wildly it is probably

○ *Picturesque St George's chapel, on top of Lykavittos*

best not to quote them, but in general it operates from about 08.45 to 24.00 or soon after, except on Thursday, when it currently does not open until 10.30. In summer it runs up and down every 10 minutes, reducing to every half-hour in the winter.

The healthier approach is to walk to the top, and it's a pleasant if sometimes steep hike up, at first under the shade of trees but later in the open – so take care on a very hot day. Partway up is a café/restaurant whose lovely view offers a good excuse for a break. At the top of the hill is a proper restaurant, with an even better view, and both these places are popular at sunset and into the evening. Also at the top of Lykavittos is the little chapel of St George (Agios Giorgios), very picturesque, and beyond that an open-air theatre, popular for both classical and rock concerts.

CULTURE

Benaki Museum

Several of the museums in Athens have a narrow focus, on folk art or ancient Greece, but the wonderful Benaki collection covers all ages, and includes a collection of Egyptian items too. This 19th-century mansion which houses the collection of over 20,000 objects, and which was impressively renovated recently, belonged to a wealthy Greek-Alexandrian cotton trader, Antoine Emmanuel Benaki, who obviously had exquisite and quite catholic tastes. Housed in chronological order on several floors are such things as Myceanean jewellery, paintings (including an El Greco) and Lord Byron's writing desk. There is even an Egyptian reception room from a 17th-century palace, and there are excellent displays on the Greek War of Independence. It's a museum not to be missed. Indeed, so vast was Benaki's collection that it now has two offshoots. There are temporary exhibitions and performances at the Pireos Street Annexe and the 8000-piece Benaki Museum of Islamic Art.

Benaki Museum ⓐ Koumbari 1/Vasilissis Sofias. ⓣ 210 367 1000. ⓦ www.benaki.gr ⓛ Wed–Mon 09.00–17.00 (closes Sun 15.00, Thur 24.00).

Pireos Street Annexe ⓐ Pireos 138. ① 210 345 3111. ① Wed–Thu
09.00–17.00, Fri–Sun 10.00–22.00.
Benaki Museum of Islamic Art ⓐ Agion Asomaton and Dipylou.
① 210 325 1311. ① Tue, Fri–Sun 09.00–15.00, Wed 09.00–21.00.

Goulandris Museum of Cycladic Greek Art

The Cycladic civilisation flourished in the Cycladic islands of the
Greek Aegean from 3200 to 2200BC. It produced some of the most
exquisite art of any period in Greek history, particularly its
beautifully graceful marble statues, which are here displayed to
great effect. You can see how they influenced more modern artists
such as Modigliani, and there are some tempting reproductions on
sale in the shop.

The core collection was amassed by the Greek shipping magnate
Nikolas P. Goulandris, who was also a great patron of the arts and
obviously a man with discerning taste. Don't miss the museum
annexe, the Stathatos Mansion, which holds temporary exhibitions
but is itself of immense interest. It was designed by, and was the
home of, Ernst Ziller, a German architect. Ziller designed many of the
best late 19th-century buildings in Athens, including the Presidential
Palace (see page 86) and the Panathenaic Stadium (see page 89.)
ⓐ Neofytou Douka 4. ① 210 722 8321. ⓦ www.cycladic.gr ① Mon and
Wed–Fri 10.00–16.00, Sat 10.00–15.00.

Byzantine Museum

This is probably a museum more for the specialist, but if you are
interested in Byzantine art and history then this is one of the best

---

▶ *The Goulandris Museum has the world's best collection of the unique and
beautiful art of the Cycladic civilisation*

collections of its kind in the world including icons, sculptures and religious items.

The main building is a villa which was built in the 1840s for the Duchesse de Plaisance. Born in Pennsylvania, she married one of Napoleon's generals, from whom she gained her title, but after his death she travelled to Greece, fell in love with the country and made Athens her home, commissioning this building. Note that the collection and the buildings that house it are being renovated at present. Following the exciting discovery that this was the site of Aristotle's Lyceum, an archaeological dig is also taking place, meaning that the museum will be closed from time to time.

ⓐ Vasilissis Sofias 22. ❶ 210 721 1027. ⏱ Tue–Sun 08.30–15.00 (but check first).

War Museum of Greece

Not as bombastic as its name might suggest, this is in fact a fascinating museum which covers the story of warfare from classical times onwards. It spreads over several floors, and extends outside, where various planes and tanks are on display. Inside there are fascinating exhibits on warfare from Mycenaean times, the campaigns of Alexander the Great, detailed models of some of Greece's fortified towns and a powerful display of life during World War II in Athens, and afterwards when the Civil War ripped the country apart. There is also an extensive collection of weaponry, especially suits of armour.

ⓐ Vasilissis Sofias 22. ❶210 725 2974. ⏱ Tue–Sun 09.00–14.00.

National Gallery

A disappointment by the standards of other European National Galleries, and in comparison to some of the other museums in

Athens, but it does have a good collection of El Greco's works and hosts major international exhibitions, so check what's on. The permanent collection has some appealing Greek landscapes, as well as works by Picasso, Rembrandt, Goya and other well-known names, though the building itself is hideously ugly.

ⓐ Vasilissis Konstantinou 50. ⓣ 210 723 5857. ⓛ Mon and Wed 09.00–15.00 and 18.00–21.00, Thu–Sat 09.00–15.00, Sun 10.00–14.00.

RETAIL THERAPY

Kolonaki is the part of Athens to head for if you want to do some designer shopping, or hunt out art works, jewellery or antiques. Here's where you'll find a Gucci boutique rubbing shoulders with names better-known in Greece such as Giorgos Eleftheriadis and the shoe designer Petridis. The shop at the Benaki Museum is a fabulous place, the best museum shop in the city, and has a great range of beautifully made reproductions of items from this fine collection.

Gucci ⓐ in the Melathron Centre at Tsakalof 5.

Giorgos Eleftheriadis ⓐ Pindarou 38.

Petridis ⓐ Platia Kolonakiou.

AFTER DARK

Rooms with a view

Head to the top of Lykavittos by funicular or on foot for the night-time view over the city. If you're planning to eat up there then footslogging it up is perhaps not the most relaxing way to arrive, especially as the restaurant at the top, Orizondes Lykavittou (see page 97) is rather swish.

Other places with a night-time view include the rooftop Galaxy Bar at the Athens Hilton (see page 36), the GB Roof Garden Restaurant at the Grande Bretagne hotel (see page 86) and the bar and Grand Balcon restaurant on top of the St George Lycabettus Hotel (ⓐ Kleomenous 2. ⓣ 210 729 0711. ⓦ www.sglycabettus.gr).

Other bars & entertainment

If you want to keep your feet on the ground there's also the Frame Bohemian Bar in the St George Lycabettus, and other good bars around include Briki Platia Mavili to the east of Lykavittos, and Mommy and En Delphis, both on Delfou – one of the streets to head for. If you can get tickets then one of the outdoor concerts at the Lykavittos Theatre (ⓣ 210 618 9300), which run roughly from May to October, is a fabulous Athenian experience.

Restaurants

Benaki Museum Café € Great place for a meal (lunch as well as dinner) on this attractive second-floor terrace, with a very popular buffet on their Thursday late-night opening, for which you would be advised to book. ⓐ Koumbari 1/Vasilissis Sofias. ⓣ 210 367 1000. ⓦ www.benaki.gr ⓛ Wed–Mon 09.00–17.00 (closes Sun 15.00, Thu 24.00).

Dexameni € Well loved and long-established café-restaurant, with mainly light meals but a great people-watching place in a lovely little Kolonaki square. ⓐ Dexameni Square. ⓣ 210 723 2834. ⓛ Daily 08.00–02.00, May–Oct only.

Ouzadiko €€ This contemporary take on a traditional Greek ouzerie shows off the new Greek-style cooking at its best with a long list of *meze*, the Greek version of tapas, to choose from, and the chance to find out that not all ouzos taste the same. ⓐ Karneadou 25-29 (in the shopping mall). ⓣ 210 729 5484. ⓛ Tue–Sat 12.30–17.30 and 20.00–24.00.

Ratka €€–€€€ International menu ranges from sushi to pasta in this chic place, which has been a fashionable meeting and eating spot in Kolonaki for decades. Haritos 32. ⓣ 210 729 0746. ⓛ Mon–Fri 09.00–02.00, Sat 13.00–17.00, Oct–May only.

Aigli Bistro Café €€€ Fabulous setting in the National Gardens by the Zappeion, but don't assume it's just another café, as the bistro-style menu is very inventive, as is the more extensive (and expensive) French-influenced evening menu. ⓐ Zappeion. ⓣ 210 336 9363. ⓛ Daily 13.00–16.30, 20.30–late.

Balthazar €€€ This has long been one of the most stylish places to eat and greet in Athens, housed in a wonderful 19th-century mansion on the north-east edge of Kolonaki. ⓐ Vournazou/Tsocha 27. ⓣ 210 644 1215. ⓛ Tue–Sat 21.00–late.

Boschetto €€€ One of the priciest places in town, but worth the splurge for the Italian nouvelle cuisine menu, noted for its seafood. One to dress up for, with seating both indoors and out. ⓐ Evangelismos. ⓣ 210 721 0893. ⓛ Mon–Sat 18.00–23.00.

Orizondes Lykavittou €€€ Rather swish and run by Greek TV celebrity chef, Yannis Geldis. Views are tremendous. ⓐ Lykavittos ⓣ 210 722 7065. ⓛ Daily 12.00–01.30.

Around Athens

Although you could spend a week or more exploring the centre of Athens on foot and not get bored, using public transport or a rental car opens up a whole other world of contrasting experiences. At either end of the city's first metro line you have the contrasting destinations of Pireas (often spelled Piraeus) and Kifissia. The first is the Mediterranean port in all its chaotic and noisy glory, the second a leafy and more refined suburb where you'll find diplomats living amid boutique hotels. You'll come across remote archaeological sites where you might be the only visitor, in total contrast to most people's experience at the Acropolis. The new metro system allows much easier access now to the historic monastery at Dafni, and the bus will allow you to join the Athenians who go out to Cape Sounion to see one of Greece's most dramatically located temples.

PIREAS

Whether you need to go there to catch a ferry or not, the port of Pireas is worth a few hours of anyone's time. There are a couple of interesting museums, a very lively flea market, the typical bustle and confusion of a busy working port and, if you're a seafood lover, some very tempting restaurants. A long Sunday lunch by the water at Pireas is a popular Athenian activity. The atmosphere that was caught in the film *Never On A Sunday*, in which Melina Mercouri played a Pireas prostitute, is definitely still here.

Culture

Archaeological Museum Though it's nowhere near as big as the National Archaeological Museum in Athens, if you're at all

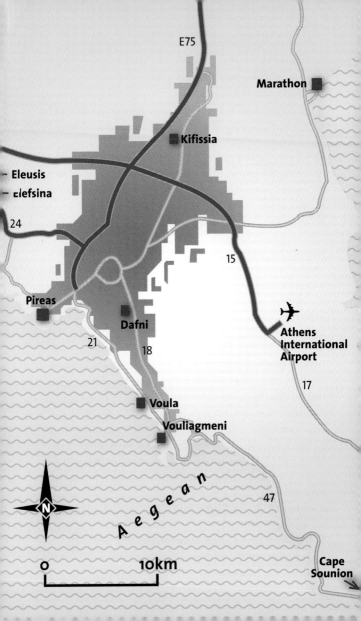

> **FERRY GOOD ADVICE**
> If you're travelling to Pireas to catch a ferry, make sure you allow plenty of time, and try to find out beforehand which harbour your boat sails from. There are several harbours in different places, and the layout of Pireas can be confusing so make sure you've got adequate time. Thomas Cook's definitive annual guide *Greek Island Hopping* is the last word on ferry ports and timetables.

interested in Greek history you should definitely head here. Many ancient Greek artefacts have been found, perfectly preserved, in the waters off Pireas, and a good number of the best objects are on display here. Also don't miss (though it's hard to) the huge grave monument the size of a small temple. ⓐ Harilaou Trikoupi 31. ⓘ 210 452 1598. ⓛ Tue–Sun 08.30–15.00. ⓜ Metro: Pireas.

Hellenic Maritime Museum With the proud naval history of Athens and Pireas, this is the perfect spot for a museum that celebrates that heritage. There are model ships from the ancient triremes through to modern battleships, displays on navigation systems (again, ancient and modern) and fascinating models of famous Greek naval battles. ⓐ Akti Themistokleous, Zea Marina. ⓘ 210 451 6264. ⓛ Tue–Sat 09.00–14.00. ⓜ Metro: Pireas.

Retail therapy
If you visit Pireas on a Sunday morning then you should definitely

ⓞ *Zea is one of the many busy harbours at Pireas*

take in the extensive flea market. This is easy to find, very close to the metro station, and while not as large as the one in central Athens, it does have its own salty atmosphere.

Restaurants

Dourabeis €€ If a seafood restaurant has been in business for over 60 years then it must be doing something right, and the secret here is … keep it simple. The freshest of fish, the lightest of grillings and dinner is perfect. Not cheap, but fish never is. ③ Akti Dilaveri 27–29. ❶ 210 412 2092. ❷ Daily 18.00–23.00. ❸ Metro: Faliro.

Jimmy and the Fish €€–€€€ Ask an Athenian to recommend one Pireas fish restaurant and chances are it would be this one, not just for the fresh fish and its speciality seafood pasta dishes but also its lovely setting on the harbour at Mikrolimano. Don't expect to turn up late on a sunny Sunday lunchtime and expect to find an empty seat. ③ Akti Koumoundourou 46. ❶ 210 412 4417. ❷ Daily 12.00–02.00. ❸ Metro: Faliro

Plous Podilatou €€€ If you want something more creative than just plain grilled fish, then Plous Podilatou is the place to find it. This restaurant specialises in seafood with a nouvelle twist and is a fairly chic place on the harbour at Mikrolimano. It's advisable to book. ③ Akti Koumoundourou 42. ❶ 210 413 7910. ❷ Daily 09.00–16.00 and 19.00–01.00. ❸ Metro: Faliro

DAFNI

There has been a monastery on this site since the 5th or 6th century, and it is worth making the journey out to these industrial suburbs to see it. The present buildings date back to an 11th-century renovation, and it is the mosaics which were created then that are the monastery's biggest attraction. It is awe-inspiring to look at the beautiful colours and designs and realise that they are almost a thousand years old. Impressive too is the church's huge dome, 8 m (26 ft) in diameter. Though it is not immensely high by cathedral standards at only 16 m (52 ft), in such a small monastery it creates a suitably reverential atmosphere. ● Daily 08.30–15.00 Ⓜ Metro: Line 2.

ELEUSIS

One Sacred Way led from Athens to Delphi (see page 123) and another led here to what was, in the 6th century BC, a sacred site to rival Delphi. It was the home of a cult of some 30,000 people, and so secret were their rituals that no records remain of what happened here. It's 16 km (10 miles) from Athens, the same distance as Kifissia, but it could hardly be more different, as this is an oil refinery suburb (modern Elefsina), with no reason to linger other than this unique site. There isn't a great deal to see, as the remains are rather overgrown, but it's a haunting place and the enjoyable and thorough museum explains and speculates on what went on here. ⓐ Gioga 1, Platia Eleusis. ⓣ 210 554 6019.
● Tue–Sun 08.30–15.00. Ⓜ Bus A16 or B16 from Platia Koumoundourou in Athens to Strofi, then short walk.

KIFISSIA

The northern suburb of Kifissia, 16 km (10 miles) away at the end of Metro Line 1, is at a higher elevation than central Athens and has therefore always been a desirable neighbourhood to live in. It's cooler at the height of summer, and these days is cooler in another way, with its gourmet restaurants and chic hotels. With its parks and leafy streets, it makes for a pleasant excursion, with its Museum of Natural History a big attraction.

Culture

The Gaia Centre This associate of both the Natural History Museum in London and the nearby Goulandris Museum is an excellent option for families. It looks at the environment by using all the latest interactive means at a modern museum's disposal, with a good balance between fun and education. 🅐 Othonos 100.
🆔 210 801 5870. 🕐 Mon–Thu and Sat 09.0–14.30, Sun 10.00–14.30.
Ⓜ Metro: Kifissia.

Goulandris Museum of Natural History Exceptionally good little museum, mainly focusing on the natural history of Greece, of course, and it might just whet your appetite to explore the country further. The displays on the country's endangered species are also illuminating, and there is a vast botanical collection said to contain in the region of 250,000 specimens. 🅐 Levidou 13. 🆔 210 801 5870.
🕐 Mon–Thu and Sat 09.00–14.30, Sun 10.00–14.30.
Ⓜ Metro: Kifissia.

Retail therapy

Pack your plastic money if going to well-heeled Kifissia, as there's lots of temptation in the many designer shops, for both men and women. There's lots of style, but few bargains.

Taking a break

There's plenty of choice here, with good options including the revered old patisserie of Varsos (**☎** Kassaveti 5 – just ask anyone if you can't find it) and the rather stylish Ammonites Café-Restaurant in the Gaia Centre.

Restaurants

Vardis €€€ If you want to impress people, even just yourself perhaps, the wonderfully grand Vardis restaurant in the Hotel Pentelikon is the place to do it. With its Michelin star (it was the first in Greece to get one) and a dining room as ornate as its menu, it is the place to eat in Kifissia. **☎** Hotel Pentelikon, Diligianni 16. **☎** 210 623 0650. **🕐** Mon–Sat 20.30–01.00 (closed Aug).

Accommodation

Kefalari Suites €€ Ultra-swish collection of 12 individually themed private suites, each coming with its own PC as well as a whirlpool. Out in the leafy suburb of Kifissia, but easy metro access to the city centre. **☎** Pentelis 1 & Kolokotroni. **☎** 210 623 3333. **🌐** www.kefalarisuites.gr

AKRA SOUNIO (CAPE SOUNION)

The 5th-century BC **Temple of Poseidon**, which sits on top of the 60 m (200 ft) high Cape Sounion, is one of the most dramatically situated sanctuaries in Greece. It's easily reached by bus or car, or you can join an organised tour. It's especially popular at sunset, when crowds troop out from Athens to see the orange sun sink into the Aegean. Note that the last bus back to Athens leaves not long after sunset, so if you want to linger you'll need to get a taxi or take one of the afternoon organised tours (see any travel agent or your hotel), which allows you time for a post-sunset sundowner before taking you back to central Athens. One noted visitor to the site was the poet Lord Byron, who came in 1810 and carved his name into one of the massive grey marble columns, of which 15 remain standing from the 34 originals. You won't get near enough today to even think of carving your name, and any attempt to do so would see you hauled off to jail. Far better to enjoy the views out to Aegina and the Peloponnese to the west, and the Cycladic island of Kea to the east.

Restaurants

There's no shortage of choice here, down on the beach or along the

● *Cape Sounion's temple of the god of the sea*

road, and the café-restaurant that's in the prime position right by the temple does good food or you can relax with just a drink.

Accommodation

Aegaeon €€ The Aegaeon is down on the beach at Cape Sounion so you have a bit of a walk up to the temple on the headland, though plenty of time to linger after the crowds have gone before going back to enjoy a meal in the hotel restaurant. It's comfortable and clean and ideal if you want to overnight here. ❸ Akra Sounio. ❶ 210 923 9262.

MARATHON

The name of Marathon is known around the world from the famous event after the battle there in 490 BC, when the messenger Pheidippides ran the 42 km (26 miles) to Athens to give the news of the Greek victory, and then collapsed and died. The Persians vastly outnumbered the Greeks, but 6400 Persians died compared to 192 Athenians. The Athenian dead are buried beneath a mound, which makes a simple but affecting memorial to them.

A car is the best way to get to Marathon, though you can do it on the bus too. Buses run hourly from the Mavromataion bus terminal in Athens, which is north of the National Archaeological Museum at the junction with Alexandras. Take any bus for Marathon and ask for the Tymvos stop. The trip takes 2 hours (half that if you're in a car). Buses run from early morning till late evening, but check return times locally.

The Marathon Museum is about 2.5 km (1¹/₂ miles) from the burial mound, near the modern village of Marathon. There isn't a great deal inside it, but above the museum is a small hill which gives a commanding view of the Plain of Marathon, worth visiting while you conjure up visions of the opposing warriors. ⓐ Plataion 114, Vranas, Marathon. ⓣ 229 405 5155. ⓛ Tue–Sun 08.00–15.00.

Restaurants

Kavouri €€ This waterside fish taverna could round off an enjoyable excursion to Marathon, after viewing the mound and museum. It's highly regarded for both its fresh fish and its *meze* selection. ⓐ Perikleous 24, Paralia Marathona. ⓣ 229 405 5243. ⓛ Daily, lunch and dinner.

ⓓ *Hydra is one of the most popular islands for excursions from Athens*

OUT OF TOWN
trips

The islands

If you have more than a couple of days in Athens, you might want to fit in a visit to some of the nearby Greek islands. It's a refreshing break from the city, which is why many Athenians take advantage of the opportunity. On summer weekends the islands and the boats can be very busy indeed, so travel during the week if you can, and book your ferry ticket in advance.

There are five islands within easy reach of the port of Pireas, although not many visitors bother with the island of Salamis (or Salamina), as it is so close to the mainland and the industry around Pireas that it doesn't give the true Greek island experience. For that you have to go a little further, into the four Argo-Saronic islands that are the main attractions for Athens: Aegina, Poros, Hydra (or Idra) and Spetses (or Spetsai).

With fast hydrofoils, these islands are very easy to get to. Aegina takes just 40 minutes, making it the most popular, while the furthest, Spetses is about 2 hours away. It makes it quite feasible to go and have lunch on Aegina, visit Spetses for the day, stay overnight and come back the next day, or visit more than one island in a day – though this rather defeats the point of going to them, to relax.

SALAMIS

Salamis is so close to the mainland, separated from the port of Pireas by only a narrow channel, that it sometimes scarcely feels like an island at all. It attracts many city commuters, and few tourists, so that in itself adds to the appeal of a visit. It's a large and wooded island and would be very appealing if set down in the middle of the Aegean. There are no specific sites as such, apart from one or two

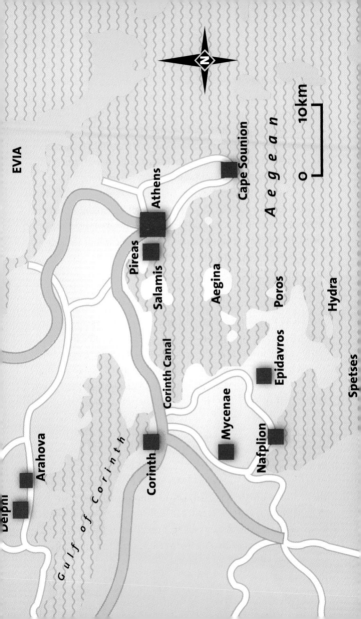

small monasteries, but there are beaches to enjoy, a few towns and villages to explore and the feel of seeing somewhere that's just that bit different.

Ferries leave from Pireas every 30 minutes between 08.00 and 17.00, and the journey takes about 45 minutes. Another ferry operates from Perama, a port to the north of Pireas (a bus service links them) and directly opposite Paloukia, the main port of Salamina. This is cheaper, takes just a few minutes, and operates between 05.00 and 24.00, should you wish to spend more time on the island. Note that there are no hotels in Paloukia or Salamina Town, so if you want to spend the night head for the smaller towns of Selinia or Eandio, where there is some accommodation and eating places.

AEGINA

If time is tight and you do want to be able to enjoy your Greek island experience, head for Aegina (also spelled Egina). Unlike Salamis this is a proper Greek holiday island, and with only a 40-minute journey to get there you can easily enjoy a full day, or even just a few hours if you're pushed for time. The capital, Aegina Town, is an attractive place with 19th-century mansions and a harbour where you'll find fishing boats bobbing and fishermen tending their nets or selling their catch by the quayside. With time to explore you can use the

🔽 *Take a ferry from Pireas to the islands*

island's bus service or taxis to visit temples and beaches. If you can stay overnight it's even better, as there are some good tavernas where you can enjoy a relaxing dinner, and accommodation is plentiful and not expensive. If you avoid midsummer weekends you should be able to find somewhere without booking ahead.

Sights & attractions

Temple of Afaia The Temple of Afaia is the island's main historical site and is easily reached from Aegina Town, being only 12 km (7 miles) to the east and served by the local bus network. It was built in the 5th century BC, and is not only older than the Parthenon but much better preserved, in fact one of the best preserved in Greece, and history buffs will want to go to Aegina for this reason alone.

The temple is close to the package holiday resort of Ayia Marina, from where you can also catch the ferry back to Pireas, but unless you prefer the full English breakfast to more authentic Greek food, you would be better off staying in Aegina Town.

🕒 Mon–Fri 08.00–19.00, Sat–Sun 08.00–15.00.

🚌 Bus from Aegina Town to Ayia Marina stops at the Temple.

Archaeological Museum The town's main museum is only small, partly because some of the island's best finds have been taken away to the National Archaeological Museum and also to the Glypothek in Munich: King Ludwig I of Bavaria bought pediments and other items off the Temple of Afaia from the Turks during their occupation of Greece. Nevertheless, enough remains to show you what a wealth of material has been found on Aegina.

After dark

If you want lively nightlife then the resort of Ayia Marina has

endless bars, clubs and discos, but the biggest disco on the island is
Vareladiko in Faros, about 3km (2 miles) south of Aegina Town.

Agora €€ The name means 'the market' and this fish taverna, right
by the fish market, is justifiably popular for its fresh fish and much
cheaper than Athens – so Athenians love it!.
ⓐ Fish market, Aegina Town. ⓣ 229 702 7308.

Accommodation
Aeginitiko Arondiko (Traditional Pension) € Delightful small hotel
in an 18th-century mansion that has been sympathetically restored,
adding modern conveniences but keeping the old-fashioned look
and antique furniture. ⓐ Thomaidou 1, Aegina Town.
ⓣ 229 702 4968. ⓕ 22970 26716.

POROS

All of these Argo-Saronic islands are attractive in their different
ways, but the harbour at Poros Town is rather special. It's quite a
deep harbour, so even big boats can tie up right on the quayside. The
town's white houses stand on a slope that falls down to the
harbour, providing quite an unusual and picturesque effect. The
island is also only a few hundred yards from the mainland, and little
boats regularly ply back and forth. If you choose to spend a day on
Poros, you can easily go across to the Peloponnese and be walking
among vast lemon groves within minutes. Poros itself is also worth
exploring, perhaps by renting a bike or moped as it is quite a
sizeable place. There is plenty of mass tourism here in summer, but
also quiet places including the ruins of the 6th-century BC Temple of
Poseidon and the lovely little Monastery of Zoödochou Pigis.

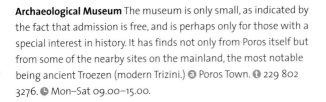

Archaeological Museum The museum is only small, as indicated by the fact that admission is free, and is perhaps only for those with a special interest in history. It has finds not only from Poros itself but from some of the nearby sites on the mainland, the most notable being ancient Troezen (modern Trizini.) ❷ Poros Town. ❶ 229 802 3276. ❸ Mon–Sat 09.00–15.00.

After dark

Poros Town gets lively at night as there are lots of holiday hotels nearby, and it's especially buzzing on the weekends when the Athenians also descend. There are plenty of bars and clubs, but the main focus is on eating out, especially down near the harbour.

Caravella €€ Right by the harbour is this justifiably popular spot, which only serves fresh fish (many places use imported frozen fish) and organically-grown vegetables. ❷ Harbour, Poros Town. ❶ 229 802 3666 ❸ Daily 11.00–late.

Accommodation

Poros Hotel €–€€ Right on the harbour is this excellent old but refurbished B-class hotel. ❷ Poros Town. ❶ 229 802 2216/22218. ❶ 229 802 5725. ❸ Apr–Oct.

HYDRA

Hydra has always been chic, the haunt of poets and artists in the 1960s. Some of that bohemian feel has lingered on, though it can be hard to find it on a busy summer's day when Athenians, day-trippers

◀ *Poros is one of the prettiest of the nearby islands*

and cruise ship passengers join the crowds of regular holidaymakers too. But it is still a wonderful harbour, surrounded by beautiful white-painted mansions. It's easy enough to walk out of the town if you have time to spare, and explore the rest of this rather rocky but attractive and virtually traffic-free island.

Sights & attractions

In Hydra Town you can buy a map which will direct you to some of the most interesting mansions, which were mainly built by architects from Venice and Genoa for the wealthy shipping merchants of Hydra. Some are private homes but others have been put to various uses. One is a students' hostel and another houses the small Historical Archives Museum and the Public Art Gallery.

Retail therapy

The island's artistic tradition has kept up and there are now numerous art galleries, and while some of these cater unashamedly to the tourist market, others have more creative works for sale. See the changing displays at **Hydra Workshops**, near the harbour.

After dark

Hydra Town is quite small and compact and the action centres round the harbourside bars, but there are a couple of discos out of town, notably **Heaven** (ⓘ 229 805 2716).

O Kypos (The Garden) €–€€ This long-standing restaurant is up in the town and you dine in the garden, which is filled with shady trees. Grilled meat is the speciality but there's plenty for fish-lovers

---

 Most of Hydra's traffic is of this variety

too. ⓐ Hydra Town. ⓣ 229 805 2329. ⓛ Daily 19.00–late.

Accommodation

Angelica €–€€ A delightful converted mansion, well worth trying to book ahead if you plan to stay as the island can get busy. ⓐ Miaouli 42, Hydra Town. ⓣ 229 805 3202. ⓕ 229 805 3698. ⓔ angelicahotel@hotmail.com

SPETSES

Covered with pine trees and dotted with monasteries, Spetses was once a wealthy island thanks to the shipping trade, and today the distinguished mansions of Spetses Town make it well worth visiting. At 2 hours from Athens, you might consider an overnight stay, if time permits. There are a couple of small local museums

worth pottering in, and it's well worth renting a bike or moped to explore the rest of the island.

Restaurants

Exedra € This excellent taverna right on the harbour is noted for its fish dishes, which go almost straight from boat to plate, but it also has exceptionally good vegetarian dishes too. ❷ Old Harbour, Spetses Town. ❶ 229 807 3497. ❸ Daily, lunch and dinner.

Accommodation

Economou €€ Fabulous 1850s sea captain's mansion, beautifully restored and right by the sea. Only a few rooms, so book ahead at busy periods. ❷ Spetses Town. ❶ 229 807 3400.

⬇ *Many island restaurants serve fresh fish straight from the boat*

North to Delphi

From Athens there are six buses a day to the centre of the universe. That is how the ancient Greeks regarded Delphi, where the famous oracle could predict the future and also offer advice on people's problems. In addition to the regular public bus service you can also easily drive the 178 km (111 miles) on good roads that skirt the edge of the Parnassos Mountains, on the slopes of which the site of ancient Delphi stands. It's an exhilarating drive, even if you do it the easy way and take one of the coach excursions which you can book in any travel agent or through most hotels.

◑ *The entrance to the ancient world's most famous oracle*

If booking a trip, try to find one which also takes in the stunning monastery at Ossios Loukas on the way to Delphi, or allows time in the nearby mountain village of Arahova, which is also recommended if you plan an overnight stay, though there are also plenty of accommodation and eating options in the modern town of Delphi too, which is much closer to the ancient site.

At Delphi you find the modern town, which is a pleasant-enough mountain village though these days mostly devoted to tourism. The ancient site of Delphi, on the edge of the town, is quite rightly a magnet for tourists and cruise-ship passengers, and on summer days both the site and the town can be crammed with visitors. Try to avoid peak periods if you can. Staying overnight in Delphi and getting to the site late in the day, or as soon as it opens next morning, is one way to beat the crowds and is easily done from Athens. If you have a car, basing yourself at nearby Arahova (see page 126) is more of a Greek mountain village experience.

DELPHI

Sights & attractions

The site of Ancient Delphi, known overall as the Sanctuary of Apollo, is quite large and sprawling, with some tucked-away corners, and it could take two hours and more if you want to see everything. You enter the site along the Sacred Way, which at one time led all the way from Athens to Delphi. On either side you will see the ruined remains of numerous memorials and treasury buildings, where pilgrims would leave their offerings, or which would be erected afterwards as thanks to the oracle. The Sacred Way zigzags its way up towards the Temple of Apollo, where the Oracle's mouthpiece, a priest, would deliver its predictions and pronouncements. The six columns that can be seen standing today were in fact repositioned to give an impression of the Temple's look and scale, as only the foundations remained when it was first uncovered. Beyond here are the remains of a theatre, and further on still, and easily missed, the impressive remains of an athletics stadium.

The theatre dates from the 4th century BC and in its prime would have held 5000 people, while the stadium was even larger with stone seating for 7000 spectators. It is up here at the back of the site, where few of the organised groups have time to venture, that you might get some peace on busy days. Behind you are the Parnassos mountains, where eagles and hawks fly, and you may have some idea of why this was regarded as the centre of the universe in ancient times. It received pilgrims from the 12th century BC right through to the 4th century AD.

Along the main road on the left, and separate from the main precinct, is the Castalian Spring, where visitors to the site had to purify themselves first. Further on still, on the other side of the road, is the Sanctuary of Athena (with free admission), Athena being worshipped as the Guardian of the Temple.

Sanctuary of Apollo ① 226 508 2312. ● Tue–Sun 07.30–18.45, Mon 08.30–14.45.

Sanctuary of Athena ① 226 508 2312 ● June–Sept daily 07.30–20.00, Oct–May 07.30–sunset.

Culture

Archaeological Museum West of the ancient site is the excellent museum, probably the best in the country outside Athens. It isn't huge but the finds that have been made here and are on display are truly fabulous. The most famous of all is a 5th-century BC bronze called The Charioteer, which is both life-size and very lifelike, its eyes of onyx giving an eerily human feel to its gaze. Nearby is a huge marble carving of three dancing women – not to be missed.

Retail therapy

The shop at the Archaeological Museum is very well-stocked with cards and reproductions of some of its exhibits. It's worth saving some time to spend there if you are on an organised tour and your departure time is fixed.

Restaurants

Taverna Arahova € Very small place serving a limited range of dishes but all are freshly made and tasty. ⓐ Pavlou kai Frederikis 50. ⓣ 226 508 24542. ⓛ Daily, dinner only.

Vakhos Taverna € It's worth eating here for the views alone down over the valley, but the food is good too and the family which runs it stick to authentic Greek dishes without pandering to international tourist tastes. ⓐ Apollonos 31. ⓣ 226 508 3186. ⓛ Mon–Sat 08.00–23.00.

Accommodation

Varonos € Small and inexpensive family hotel with large well-appointed rooms. ⓐ Pavlou kai Frederikis 27. ⓣ 226 508 2345. ⓕ 226 508 2345.

Amalia Hotel €€ It's the best hotel in town and there are many cheaper options, but it's worth a splurge for its fabulous views down the valley at the top of which Delphi stands. ⓐ Apollonos 1. ⓣ 226 508 2101. ⓕ 226 508 2290.

OSIOS LOUKAS

On the road to Delphi, just before you get to Arahova, is the turning for the short diversion to the monastery of Osios Loukas, one of the finest in Greece. The turning is at what is known as the Oedipus crossroads, as it is here that Oedipus, returning from Delphi, is said to have murdered his father.

The monastery is easily reached if you have your own car, and some of the trips from Athens to Delphi also stop off here, but it isn't really feasible to do it on public transport from Athens on a short visit. It takes a few changes of bus, or combination of bus rides, walk or taxi ride to get to Osios Loukas. The remote location is one of its attractions, another being the mosaics and frescoes in the churches here. There are two main churches which are actually joined with a common wall and which date back to the 10th and 11th centuries. There are several other buildings, including an atmospheric little crypt with more frescoes, and a small community of monks does still live here. Osios Loukas is a very special place, and once you have been there you will never forget the visit.

ARAHOVA

The small town of Arahova is the last you pass through before reaching Delphi, and many of the tour buses stop here as the main street is lined with shops. These sell rugs, leather goods and other items made in the town or in the nearby Parnassos mountains and other parts of Greece. You need to look carefully if you want to find hand-made items, and usually the price is a good indicator. You can also buy wine, honey and other hearty mountain fare.

Arahova seems much more of a real mountain community than

🔺 *Glittering mosaics are one of the attractions of Osios Loukas*

Delphi, and when the last tour bus has passed through, it gets back to its normal life. In the evening people stroll the streets and sit in the cafés, and there's a good choice of eating places, and accommodation too.

Restaurants

Karathanassi € Offering a roof terrace in summer and a homely interior when the mountain weather gets colder, this old favourite serves real mountain food, with robust local wine. 🅐 Delfion 56. 🅣 226 703 1360. 🅛 Daily, all day.

Accommodation

Apollon Inn € Excellent, inexpensive little hotel, fairly new and well appointed, on the main street through town. 🅐 Delfion 20. 🅣 226 703 1427.

Arahova Inn € In a rather unexciting modern building, this is a comfortable and convenient C-class hotel, with all 42 rooms having balconies and different mountain views. 🅐 Arahova. 🅣 226 703 1353/2195/2196/1497. 🅕 226 703 1134. 🅔 arah_inn@otenet.gr

South to Nafplion

Lucky are those who are able to spend some time outside Athens, even if only for one or two days. A journey into the Peloponnese, to visit Greece's former capital of Nafplion and stop off at some of the stunning historical sites on the way, is to discover just how beautiful and varied the Greek mainland is. Most visitors head for the islands, understandably, but the lesser-known mainland has so much to offer. Even on this easy day trip, you can take in the Corinth canal, the stunning ancient theatre at Epidavros, the reputed tomb of King Agamemnon at Mycenae, and wind up in one of the loveliest coastal towns in Greece, Nafplion.

Some day trips from Athens will take in many or even all of these places, and you can visit one or more of them using public transport. But the best option is to drive, as you may well want to spend more time at some of these places than a coach tour or public transport timetables allow.

The furthest from Athens is Nafplion, about 146 km (91 miles) away. Driving it should be a 2-hour journey, but this depends on how

THOSE NAMES AGAIN

You might see Nafplion written as Nafplio, Navplion, Navplio, Nauplion or Nauplio. Corinth in Greek is Korinthos and Mycenae is Mikines. Epidavros might be rendered in the Roman alphabet as Epidauros, Epidavrus or Epidaurus. If catching the bus from Athens you will see the names in both Greek and Roman letters, but if using local buses you might want to swot up on your Greek alphabet first.

long it takes you to get out of Athens. There are hourly buses from
Athens to Nafplion, and you should allow about 3 hours for the
journey, with traffic and stops on the way. You can also catch a bus
to Mycenae and to Corinth, though not to Epidavros. For this you
will need to go to Nafplion and change, and there are several bus
connections each day from Nafplion to Mycenae and to Epidavros. If
you want to stop and see the Corinth Canal, you will need to drive or
join an organised tour.

NAFPLION

Nafplion is one of the most appealing towns in Greece, perhaps even
in Europe. It has a lovely waterfront, a fine headland with wonderful
views, several fortresses, a couple of interesting museums, an
offshore island to admire and a sophisticated feel, with some new
chic hotels and so many good restaurants that, no matter how long
you can manage to stay, you'll wish you were here for longer.

Sights & attractions

The massive 18th-century Venetian citadel of **Palamidi Fortress** is so
large that there are several others in ruins inside it. You can drive up
to the entrance if you have a car, but otherwise it's a steep climb up
almost 1000 steps to get there, which indicates how much the
fortress dominates the town. There isn't that much to see when you
get inside, other than the walls and some ruins, but the views are
really impressive. ☎ 275 202 8036. ⏰ Daily 08.30–18.30.

Culture

Archaeological Museum This small but fascinating collection
occupies two floors of a splendid 18th – century Venetian warehouse

129

on the town's main square. It's worth visiting to see some of the Mycenae finds that haven't been sent to the National Archaeological Museum in Athens. ➋ Platia Syntagmatos. ➊ 275 202 7502. ⏱ Tue–Sun 08.30–15.00.

Folklore Museum The Peloponnesian Folk Foundation runs this very impressive specialist little museum, one of the best in the country in dealing with local crafts and culture. It has a large collection of traditional costumes, household and agricultural items, fascinating old photographs and an excellent handicrafts shop. ➋ Ipsillantou 1. ➊ 275 202 8379. ⏱ Wed–Mon 09.00–15.00.

Retail therapy

For a small town, Nafplion has some very good shopping. Explore the back streets of the old town and you'll find potters, painters and

jewellers making and selling their wares, some good bookshops and a more upmarket kind of souvenir shop.

After dark

Nafplion is not a party town, more the kind of place where people take their evening stroll, known as the *volta*, and then go home again, leaving the visitors to enjoy themselves in the restaurants. There are some late-night bars and cafés if you want to finish the evening off with a nightcap or two, but don't expect to be dancing till dawn.

Restaurants

Karamanlis € An old favourite of the locals, and of the visitors who find it tucked away on its pedestrianised street, this is a traditional

● *Sunset transforms Nafplion's harbour*

taverna which does simple but excellent and inexpensive dishes, especially those cooked in its old ovens. ⓐ Bouboulinas 1. ❶ 275 202 7668. ❷ Daily 11.00–23.00.

Accommodation

Hotel Kapodistriou €–€€ One of the less expensive and more traditional options is this converted and comfortable old house, right in the town. ⓐ Kokinou 20. ❶ 275 202 9366. ⓦ www.hotelkapodistriou.gr

Candia House €€€ Typical of the boutique hotels that have opened here in the last few years, this exclusive little place is 20 km (12 miles) outside the town, right by the beach, with its own gym, sauna, restaurant and suites with every comfort. Chic but not cheap. ⓐ Candia House, Candia, Ireon, Nafplion. ❶ 275 209 4060. ❶ 275 209 4480. ⓦ www.candiahouse.gr

CORINTH

There are really four Corinths, and you'll need some time to explore them all so you will need to do some planning. Most people want to see the Corinth Canal, that engineering wonder that effectively turned the Peloponnese into an island by severing it from the rest of mainland Greece. It was built in what had long been a strategic spot, but this is now a few kilometres from the centre of modern Corinth, which in turn is a few kilometres from the site of Ancient Corinth, though a regular bus service connects town and site. The high citadel of Acrocorinth is close to Ancient Corinth as the crow flies, but the crow is lucky as the human has to climb a steep 4 km

❷ *The views from Nafplion's Palamidi Fortress are worth the 1000-step climb*

(2¹/₂ miles) or take a taxi to get there. Modern Corinth is a rather uninspiring town, and though there are hotels and restaurants if you need to spend the night, the charms of Nafplion are little more than an hour's drive away, so head there for the evening.

Sights & attractions

Acrocorinth There is no charge to visit the original ancient acropolis of Corinth, with its 2 km (1 mile) of walls on top of a huge rocky hill. Inside are the remains of a later Turkish fortress, and evidence of others who have invaded Greece and fortified this powerful spot. For today's visitor the main delight is to see the stunning views over the plains around and the Gulf of Corinth. ◗ Daily 08.00–19.00 (15.00 in winter).

Ancient Corinth It's hard to believe now but this site was once a city with a population of 300,000 citizens and a further 460,000 slaves. The parts that have been excavated are interesting, with a vast market place and the remnants of a 5th-century BC Temple of Apollo, but what has been uncovered is a tiny fraction of what was originally here. There's also an Archaeological Museum within the site. ❶ 274 103 1207. ◗ Daily 08.00–19.00 (17.00 in winter).

Corinth Canal Twelve years of work had gone into the Corinth Canal when it was completed in 1893 (having been mooted for a few thousand years). It really is an awe-inspiring sight, especially if you are lucky enough to stand on the road bridge over the canal when a ship is passing through. There is nothing much else to do, once you've admired it for a while, so don't set aside too much time for it.

◗ *The Corinth Canal cuts mainland Greece in two*

EPIDAVROS

The ancient theatre at Epidavros – easily the finest in Greece – is one of the country's greatest attractions, ranking alongside the Acropolis and the Palace at Knossos in Crete. To see it empty is impressive enough, but if you are lucky enough to attend one of the summer performances here the effect is truly magical. The theatre dates back to the 4th century BC and can seat 14,000 people in its 55 rows of seats. The acoustics are said to be perfect, and from the back row you can hear people talking in the centre of the stage, way below. Amazingly enough, the theatre fell into disuse, eventually became overgrown and – though it's hard to imagine it now – was lost until rediscovered at the end of the 19th century and fully restored in all its glory in 1954.

Dramatic in every sense – the Theatre of Asklepios at Epidavros

Epidavros Festival Ⓦ www.greekfestival.gr Ⓛ July–Aug. Tickets bookable through website.

The theatre is only part of a much larger site, so allow at least an hour for a visit. Medical practitioners were based at Epidavros, and drama was one of the cures they used for the mental and physical ailments which were brought to them here. There are also the remains of a bathhouse, a gymnasium and the guesthouse where people stayed when they visited. There is also an **Archaeological Museum** within the site, displaying its finds. Look for the medical instruments, and be glad you weren't around at the time.

There is a hotel near the site if you wish to stay the night, but it's not a very exciting place to spend the evening unless there's a performance on. A far better option is to head to Nafplion, about a 40-minute drive away. There are also several buses each day.

MYCENAE

There have been people living on this site since at least 6000 BC, but it was during the Mycenaean period, in the 16th–13th centuries BC, that the palace here was at its peak. It was said to be the home of Agamemnon, whose name appears in Homer and who may have been a real Mycenaean king. The site was excavated in the 19th century by the German archaeologist Heinrich Schliemann, who uncovered the gold mask and other fabulous treasures now on display in the National Archaeological Museum in Athens. On finding the mask Schliemann sent a telegram to the King of Greece which said, 'I have gazed upon the face of Agamemnon!' He hadn't, as the dates later proved to be wrong, but the site, with its entrance under the famous Lion Gate, continues to fascinate. ❶ 275 107 6585. ⏱ Daily 08.00–19.00 (winter 15.00).

Restaurants

La Belle Helene €€ There are several places which cater to the lunchtime tourist trade, but the restaurant attached to the Belle Helene hotel (see below) is open all year round.
ⓐ Mycenae. ❶ 275 107 6225. ⏱ Daily, lunch and dinner.

Accommodation

La Belle Helene € This is the best of the limited accommodation options near Mycenae, and is where Heinrich Schliemann stayed, so you can't fault it for historical atmosphere, though it is quite basic. Check the visitors' book, which bears such names as Debussy and Virginia Woolf. ⓐ Mycenae. ❶ 275 107 6225. ❶ 27510 76179.

● *Athens International Airport is most visitors' gateway to the city*

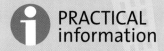

PRACTICAL
information

Directory

GETTING THERE

By air

Eleftherios Venizelos International Airport has direct flights from London Heathrow with British Airways and with the Greek national carrier Olympic Airways, and from Gatwick and Luton with the budget airline Easyjet. There are also direct flights with Olympic from New York, Boston, Montreal, Toronto and Melbourne. Delta also flies daily from New York to Athens. Many US carriers fly via other European cities including London, Paris and Amsterdam.

British Airways Ⓦ www.ba.com

Olympic Airways Ⓦ www.olympicairlines.com

Easyjet Ⓦ www.easyjet.com

By rail

You have to really want to take the train to Athens, when flying is much more convenient and cheaper, unless you are already in south-east Europe on a railpass holiday. To get there by rail from London you must take the Eurostar to Paris (3 hours) and change there for the 24-hour onward journey to Brindisi in Italy. In Brindisi you can catch a ferry to Patras on the Greek mainland, and from here catch a train again to Athens. It takes 2–3 days altogether, and is really only advisable if you want to break the journey at the stops on the way. For more details, consult the *Thomas Cook European Rail Timetable* and Thomas Cook's *Greek Island Hopping*.

Eurostar Reservations (UK) ❶ 08705 186 186. Ⓦ www.eurostar.com

Thomas Cook European Rail Timetable ❶ (UK) 01733 416477; (USA) 1 800 322 3834. Ⓦ www.thomascookpublishing.com

Driving

The most scenic and practical route from the UK is to cross the
Channel and then drive down through France and Switzerland into
Italy, heading for any of the Italian ferry ports which serve Greece:
Ancona, Bari, Brindisi and Venice. These will take you to Patras in the
Peloponnese, Greece's third-largest city, from where it is a 2–3 hour
drive to Athens. Allow four days for the journey. Driving through the
countries of former Yugoslavia is a longer and more difficult option.

TRAVEL INSURANCE

Visitors from the UK are covered by reciprocal EU health schemes
while in Greece. You must carry with you the new European Health

Pireas is the hub of Greece's extensive ferry system

Insurance Card (EHIC). This covers free emergency treatment but does not mean that all medical expenses are free, so you will still need your regular travel insurance too. All non-EU travellers should make sure that they have adequate travel insurance.

ENTRY FORMALITIES
Documentation
Visitors to Athens from EU countries, the USA, Canada, Australia and New Zealand need only a valid passport to enter Greece. EU citizens can stay for an unlimited length of time, but cannot work without a residence permit. Others can stay for up to three months (two months for South African citizens).

Customs
Citizens of other EU countries can bring with them personal possessions along with a reasonable amount of alcohol and tobacco provided they are for personal use only and have been bought tax-paid in other EU countries. Non-EU residents, EU visitors arriving from a non-EU country and EU residents with duty-free goods can bring in 200 cigarettes, 50 cigars or 250 g of tobacco; one litre of spirits or four litres of wine; 250 ml of cologne or 50 ml of perfume.

Entry to Greece is usually very quick and informal, but one thing to note is that there is a very strong anti-drugs policy. This extends to some medicines, including codeine and some tranquilisers, which are widely available in the rest of the world. In these cases you should bring your written prescription with you, and enough medication to last for your visit.

MONEY
The euro (€) is the official currency in Greece. €1 = 100 cents. There

are notes in denominations of €5, €10, €20, €50, €100, €200 and €500, and coins in denominations of 1, 2, 5, 10, 20 and 50 cents, and €1 and €2.

There are ATM machines at the airport and throughout the city, accepting most international credit cards, the Cirrus and Plus networks being the most widely used. If you have one of these cards you should have no trouble getting cash out of an ATM. Instructions are usually available in several languages. You can also exchange travellers' cheques in banks and bureaux de change throughout the city centre on production of your passport, and some larger hotels, restaurants and shops will also take them in payment for services, though this is not universal, so don't assume it without checking first.

HEALTH, SAFETY & CRIME

The tap water in Athens is safe to drink but many people prefer to drink bottled water. It's not for reasons of safety but becomes a habit in a country where some islands can have water shortages at the end of a long, hot summer.

Medical facilities in Greece are generally good, but the free medical help can be quite basic and you should definitely carry insurance to cover any extra costs you might incur. For minor ailments and general medical advice, many people use the pharmacies: look for the green cross symbol (see page 154 for further details). Pharmacists are highly trained and often speak English and other languages.

Athens is generally a very safe city indeed, but don't be lulled into a false sense of security. The chances of having a bad experience are very low, but that doesn't mean you should leave common sense at home. There are still pickpockets and petty thieves about, so watch your possessions. Ignore anyone who approaches you on the street and engages you in conversation, usually by asking you the time. They may be harmless and touting for business for a hotel, but they may also be con-men. Avoid deserted streets late at night: the area around Omonia Square was always a place to avoid in the small hours, though it has been cleaned up a lot in recent years.

Throughout Greece there is a separate branch of the police force called the Tourist Police. They are not merely a PR exercise to help lost tourists but have very strong and wide-ranging powers. They inspect and grade hotels and restaurants, set prices, have lists of accommodation options, will resolve disputes with overcharging taxi drivers, help recover lost property. and will help you if you yourself get lost. In case of any problems with anything to do with your visit, short of serious crime, your first port of call should be the Tourist Police (☎ 171). For contact details of police, see page 154.

OPENING HOURS
Shops

Hours vary widely with the shop and with the season. Most shops usually open about 08.00/09.00 and stay open till about 15.00 on Mon/Wed/Sat, and are also open from 17.00–20.00 on Tue/Thu/Fri. Department stores and souvenir shops tend to stay open all day, and in the summer months souvenir shops will also be open on Sundays.

Banks

Most banks are open 08.00–14.30 from Monday to Thursday, and 08.00–13.30 or 14.00 on Friday. If you want to change money, plenty of bureaux de change stay open all day, every day, but exchange rates will not be as good.

TOILETS

There are very few public toilets in Athens, and they are best avoided. Many larger stores have them, as do the bigger fast-food outlets, and no one will mind if you want to use them. If you wish to use the facilities at a restaurant, café or bar, it is only polite to ask someone first. They seldom object.

CHILDREN

Greeks love children and even in busy Athens restaurants there will be time to make a fuss of them, especially the children of visitors. In family-run establishments it's not unusual for a young guest to be whisked away to the kitchen where grandmother or auntie will entertain them. Greek children frequently eat out with the adults, and if there are several of them they may even have their own separate table. It's easy to get child portions too.

There is no problem buying supplies of nappies, baby food or anything else for babies and young children, as there are plenty of supermarkets and neighbourhood shops which stock them. From a health point of view you may prefer to provide them with bottled water rather than tap water. It's obvious in summer that they will need sun protection, but don't forget it at other times, too. The Mediterranean sun can burn even on overcast days.

Many attractions have reduced admission rates for children, though there's no consistency about the ages covered. At most government-run sites and museums, under-18s are admitted free. There are reduced rates on public transport too. Most hotels will allow one or more children (depending on bed space) to share their parents' room free of charge, though there may be a charge for breakfast.

Contrary to what you might expect in such an ancient city, there

is plenty to keep children entertained too. Some suggestions
include:

- **The Museum of Greek Children's Art** Right in the Plaka, this
  museum has exhibitions of art from children all over Greece, and
  also has workshops that anyone can join. There is also a room
  provided with tables, papers, crayons and paints which children
  are welcome to use – popular on rainy days! ⓐ Kodrou 9. ⓣ 210
  331 2621. ⓛ Tue–Sat 10.00–14.00, Sun 11.00–14.00, closed Aug.
  ⓜ Metro: Syntagma.

- **The Greek Children's Museum** Not far from the Children's Art
  museum is this place, which is not huge but manages to cram a
  lot of fun, educational, interactive items into the space. The
  language barrier is not a huge problem, when you're seeing how
  the Athens metro was built or how the human eye works. Note
  that the opening hours change regularly, so you may want to
  check first.
  ⓐ Kydathineon 14. ⓣ 210 331 2995. ⓛ Tue–Fri 10.00–14.00,
  Sat–Sun 10.00–15.00. ⓜ Metro: Syntagma.

- **Foundation of the Hellenic World** One of the city's newer
  attractions in the redeveloped area of Gazi is this huge place,
  which uses multimedia and virtual reality to tell the great
  dramatic stories of ancient Greece. ⓐ Pireas 254. ⓣ 210 483 5300.
  ⓦ www.fhw.gr
  ⓛ Mon/Tue/Thu 09.00–16.00, Wed 09.00–19.00, Sat/Sun
  11.00–15.00 summer; Mon/Tue 09.00–14.00, Wed/Thu/Fri
  09.00–21.00, Sun 10.00–15.00 winter. ⓜ Metro: Kalithea.

- **The Museum of Greek Musical Instruments** Children love the fact that they can go from case to case, putting on headphones and hearing the different instruments. See page 70.

- **The War Museum** There are plenty of planes and tanks outside the museum that children can look into and even climb into. See page 94.

- **The Fun Train** Just as you get in many holiday resorts, a little train operates daily in the summer months.

- **The beaches** If children need to be persuaded to go into the museums, bribe them with the promise of at least one day at the beach. See page 32.

COMMUNICATIONS
Phones

The area code for Athens is 210, and this must be dialled before the number even if calling from another 210 number. Phone numbers throughout Greece have changed several times over the past few years, and now all numbers begin with a '2'. If you see a number which begins with the more conventional '0', it is probably from an old source. Mobile phone numbers begin with a '6'. If you have international roaming on your mobile you should have no trouble using it in Athens, where every inhabitant lives with a mobile phone clamped to his or her ear.

To dial Greece from abroad, dial your international access code, generally 00, then the country code for Greece, which is 30, followed by the full 10-digit number. The old practice of dropping the first '0' has disappeared with the advent of the codes beginning with '2'. To

● *Despite the spread of mobiles, public phone booths are still busy*

dial overseas from within Athens dial oo followed by your own
country's code (UK 44, Republic of Ireland 353, USA and Canada 1,
Australia 61, New Zealand 64, South Africa 27) and then the number,
but dropping the first 'o' of the area code if there is one.

Public phone boxes are everywhere in Athens but you will need
to buy a phone card to use them, as they do not accept coins. You
can buy these at post offices and at the little kiosks which are found
throughout Athens and everywhere else in Greece. At some of these
you may be able to make a call using the kiosk's metered phone and
pay in cash, although these are becoming less common with the
increased use of mobile phones. You can also make calls at offices of

the OTE (Hellenic Telecommunications Organisation), which you'll find throughout the city. Find yourself an international booth, make the call and then pay at the desk afterwards.

Post

There are post offices all over Athens, easily spotted by their blue and yellow signs. Post boxes are bright yellow. You can buy stamps at many kiosks as well as post offices, and shops which sell postcards often also sell stamps but sometimes at a slight premium. Postcards should take 4–5 days to reach the UK and Ireland, twice as long to get to the USA, Canada, Australia and New Zealand. The current cost of sending a postcard anywhere in the world is €0.65.

Post offices are normally open Mon–Fri 08.00–15.00, but there are four main offices in central Athens which are open 08.00–20.00 Mon–Fri, Sat 08.00–14.00 and Sun 09.00–14.00. The most central of all is the one at the south-west corner of Syntagma Square, and the others are at Eolou 100, Koumoundourou 29 and Tritis Septemvriou 28.

Internet

Many of the more modern hotels have internet access in their rooms but, if not, you will have no trouble finding an internet café. There is an Easy internet Café right on Syntagma Square, the Skynet Internet Centre nearby at Voulis 30 and Arcade is also close to Syntagma at Stadiou 5. Others are close to Omonia Square and in the Plaka. Costs are cheap.

ELECTRICITY

The current in Greece is 220V and appliances use continental-style

2-pin plugs. UK appliances will only need an adaptor for the plug, readily available in electrical stores and supermarkets. US appliances designed to run on 110V will need a transformer and you should bring this with you, as they are not as easy to find.

MEDIA & LISTINGS

International newspapers are widely available, usually on the day of publication, especially around Syntagma Square and Omonia Square. The English-language *Athens Daily News* is also easily found, and its Friday edition has good listings for weekend entertainment. The *International Herald Tribune* carries an insert called *Kathimerini* that also has entertainment and event listings. Other publications to look out for include *Athinorama* and *Time Out Athens*.

TRAVELLERS WITH DISABILITIES

Athens is not a good city if you have trouble getting around. Archaeological sites have not generally been made wheelchair-accessible, and only the more recently renovated museums will have wheelchair access. Even the city streets make life hard, as does the public transport, which in theory has all been made wheelchair-accessible, but try telling that to a busy driver on a crowded bus. The only bright spot is that the newer and refurbished hotels took the chance with the Olympics coming to upgrade their facilities and become much more accessible. Useful sources of advice are:

RADAR The principal UK forum and pressure group for people with disabilities. ⓐ 12 City Forum, 250 City Road, London EC1V 8AF. ⓣ (020) 7250 3222. ⓦ www.radar.org.uk

SATH (Society for Accessible Travel & Hospitality) advises US-based travellers with disabilities. 🄰 347 Fifth Ave, Suite 610, New York, NY 10016. ☏ (212) 447 7284. 🄵 (212) 725 8253. 🆆 www.sath.org

TOURIST INFORMATION
Tourist offices

Old habits die hard and the public face of the Greek National Tourist Organisation (GNTO), in Athens at least, has always been good at doling out glossy leaflets and less good at providing the answers to visitors' questions. 'You want to get to Delphi? Well, here is a colourful leaflet with some pretty pictures.' The situation has improved since the Olympics, but you are still better advised to do your research before leaving home and take as much information with you as you can.

Airport There is a GNTO desk in the Arrivals Hall at the airport. ☏ 210 354 5101. 🕓 Mon–Fri 09.00–19.00, Sat & Sun 10.00–15.00.

Central Athens The main branch in Athens keeps moving but at time of writing was to be found on the edge of the Plaka, opposite the Zappeion. 🄰 Amalias 26A. ☏ 210 331 0392. 🕓 Mon–Fri 09.00–20.00, Sat & Sun 10.00–18.00.

Useful websites

www.athensguide.com
www.athensnews.gr
www.culture.gr
www.cultureguide.gr
www.gnto.co.uk
www.gnto.gr
www.greektourism.com

Useful phrases

These Greek words and phrases may come in handy. See also the phrases for specific situations in other parts of the book.

English	Greek	Approx. pronunciation
BASICS		
Yes	Ναι	Ne
No	Οχι	Ohi
Please	Παρακαλώ	Parakalo
Thank you	Ευχαριστώ	Efharisto
Hello	Γειά σας	Ya sas
Goodbye	Χαίρετε	Herete
Excuse me	Με συγχωρείτε	Me sinhorite
Sorry	Συγγνώμη	Signomi
That's okay	Εντάξει	Entaxi
To	Προς	Pros
From	Από	Apo
I don't speak Greek	Δεν μιλώ Ελληνικά	Den milo Ellinika
Do you speak English?	Μιλάτε Αγγλικά;	Milate Anglika?
Good morning	Καλημέρα	Kalimera
Good afternoon	Χαίρετε	Herete
Good evening	Καλησπέρα	Kalispera
Goodnight	Καληνύχτα	Kalinihta
My name is ...	Ονομάζομαι ...	Onomazome ...
DAYS & TIMES		
Monday	Δευτέρα	Deftera
Tuesday	Τρίτη	Triti
Wednesday	Τετάρτη	Tetarti
Thursday	Πέμπτη	Pembti
Friday	Παρασκευή	Paraskevi
Saturday	Σάββατο	Savvato
Sunday	Κυριακή	Kiriaki
Morning	Πρωί	Proi
Afternoon	Απόγευμα	Apoyevma
Evening	Βράδυ	Vradi
Night	Νύχτα	Nihta
Yesterday	Χτες	Htes

English	Greek	Approx. pronunciation
Today	Σήμερα	Simera
Tomorrow	Αύριο	Avrio
What time is it?	Τί ώρα είναι;	Ti ora ine?
It is ...	Είναι ...	Ine ...
09.00	Εννέα	Ennea
Midday	Μεσημέρι	Mesimeri
Midnight	Μεσάνυχτα	Mesanihta

NUMBERS

One	Ενα	Ena
Two	Δύο	Dio
Three	Τρία	Tria
Four	Τέσσερα	Tessera
Five	Πέντε	Pente
Six	Εξι	Exi
Seven	Επτά	Epta
Eight	Οκτώ	Okto
Nine	Εννέα	Ennea
Ten	Δέκα	Deka
Eleven	Εντεκα	Endeka
Twelve	Δώδεκα	Dodeka
Twenty	Είκοσι	Ikosi
Fifty	Πενήντα	Peninta
One hundred	Εκατό	Ekato

MONEY

I would like to change these traveller's cheques/this currency	Θα ήθελα να εξαργυρώσω αυτές τις ταξιδιωτικές επιταγές/ αυτό το συνάλλαγμα	Tha ithela na exaryiroso aftes tis taxidiotik esepitayes/afto to sinallagma
Do you accept credit cards?	Δέχεστε πιστωτικές κάρτες;	Deheste pistotikes kartes?

SIGNS & NOTICES

Airport	Αεροδρόμιο	Aerodromio
Rail station	Σιδηροδρομικός Σταθμός	Sidirodromikos Stathmos
Smoking/non-smoking	Για Καπνιστές/ Για μη καπνιστές	Ya kapnistes/ ya mi kapnistes
Toilets	Αποχωρητήρια	Apohoritiria
Ladies/Gentlemen	Γυναικών/Ανδρών	Yinekon/Andron
Subway	Υπόγειος Σιδηρόδρομος	Ipoyios Sidirodromos

Emergencies

EMERGENCY NUMBERS

The following are national free emergency numbers:

Ambulance 166

SOS Doctors (see page 156) 1016

Fire 199

Police 100

Tourist Police 171

Roadside Assistance 10400.

Athens Police Headquarters This is also the HQ of the Tourist Police, ❸ Alexandras 173 in the Ambelokipi district, just to the north side of Likavittos Hill. ❶ 210 951 5111 (regular police); 210 647 6000 (tourist police). Ⓜ Metro: Ambelokipi.

LOST PROPERTY

There is a Lost Property Office in the Arrivals Hall at the airport (❶ 210 353 0000). If you lose anything in the city, first go back to anywhere you think you may have left it. Most Athenians are incredibly honest and will hand things in to the owners of the establishments. Otherwise there is a Lost Property Department at the Tourist Police headquarters.

MEDICAL SERVICES

Pharmacies

In Athens pharmacies are indicated by a green cross, and are generally open Mon–Fri 08.00–14.00 and also 17.30–20.30 Tue/Thu/Fri. Outside these hours, and at weekends, a number of emergency pharmacies will be open. These rotate duties and details

EMERGENCY PHRASES

Help!	**Fire!**	**Stop!**
Βοήθεια!	Πυρκαγιά!	Σταματήστε!
Voithia!	*Pirkaya!*	*Stamatiste!*

Call an ambulance/a doctor/the police/the fire service!
Τηλεφωνήστε για ασθενοφόρο/γιατρό/αστυνομία/την πυροσβεστική!
Tilefoniste yia asthenoforo/yatro/astinomia/tin pirosvestiki!

of the nearest open pharmacies will be given in any pharmacy window or in the newspapers, or can be found by ringing 1434.

Hospitals

Greece provides free medical care, but see advice on health insurance, page 141. For an ambulance, ring 166. Several hospitals in and around the city provide 24-hour accident and emergency service including:

● *Pharmacies – look for the green cross*

Alexandra General Hospital This is close to the centre, in Kolonaki, on the main road past the War Museum. Vasilissis Sofias 80. 210 338 1100. Metro: Megaro Mousikis.

Emergency doctors & dentists

A service called **SOS Doctors** operates in Athens, providing 24-hour house-calls for a flat fee of €80 (or €100 from 23.00 to 07.00 and on public holidays). Ring the free number and the nearest on-duty doctor or dentist will be paged and sent to you. 1016.

CONSULATES & EMBASSIES

Australian Embassy Soutsou 37/Tsocha 24. 210 870 4000. 210 646 6595. www.ausemb.gr

British Embassy Ploutarchou 1. 210 727 2600. 210 727 2876 www.british-embassy.gr

Canadian Embassy Ioannou Gennadiou 4. 210 727 3400. 210 727 3480. www.athens.gc.ca

New Zealand Consulate Kifisias 268. 210 687 4700. 210 687 4444

Republic of Ireland Embassy Vasilissis Konstantinou 5–7. 210 723 2771. 210 729 3383.

South African Embassy Kifisias 60. 210 610 6645. 210 610 6640 www.southafrica.gr

US Embassy Vasilissis Sofias 91. 210 721 2951. 210 645 6282 www.usembassy.gr

Call 100 for these guys

The publishers would like to thank the following individuals for their contribution in the production of this book:

M.E.S.O. Music Events, Greece: page 10.
A1 Pix: page 13.
Mike Gerrard: pages 43, 70, 80, 93, 101, 109, 112, 116, 119, 120, 122, 127, 130, 133, 135 & 137.
Tony Gervais all other pages.

Copy-editor: Stephen York
Proofreader: Stuart McLaren

Send your thoughts to
books@thomascook.com

- **Found a great bar, club, shop or must-see sight that we don't feature?**

- **Like to tip us off about any information that needs a little updating?**

- **Want to tell us what you love about this handy little guidebook and more importantly how we can make it even handier?**

Then here's your chance to tell all! Send us ideas, discoveries and recommendations today and then look out for your valuable input in the next edition of this title. As an extra 'thank you' from Thomas Cook Publishing, you'll be automatically entered into our exciting monthly prize draw.

Email the above address (stating the book's title) or write to: CitySpots Project Editor, Thomas Cook Publishing, PO Box 227, Unit 15/16, Coningsby Road, Peterborough PE3 8SB, UK.